# STEVE PARISH

# AMAZING FACTS

## ABOUT AUSTRALIAN

# LANDSCAPES

## Text: Allan Fox

# Contents

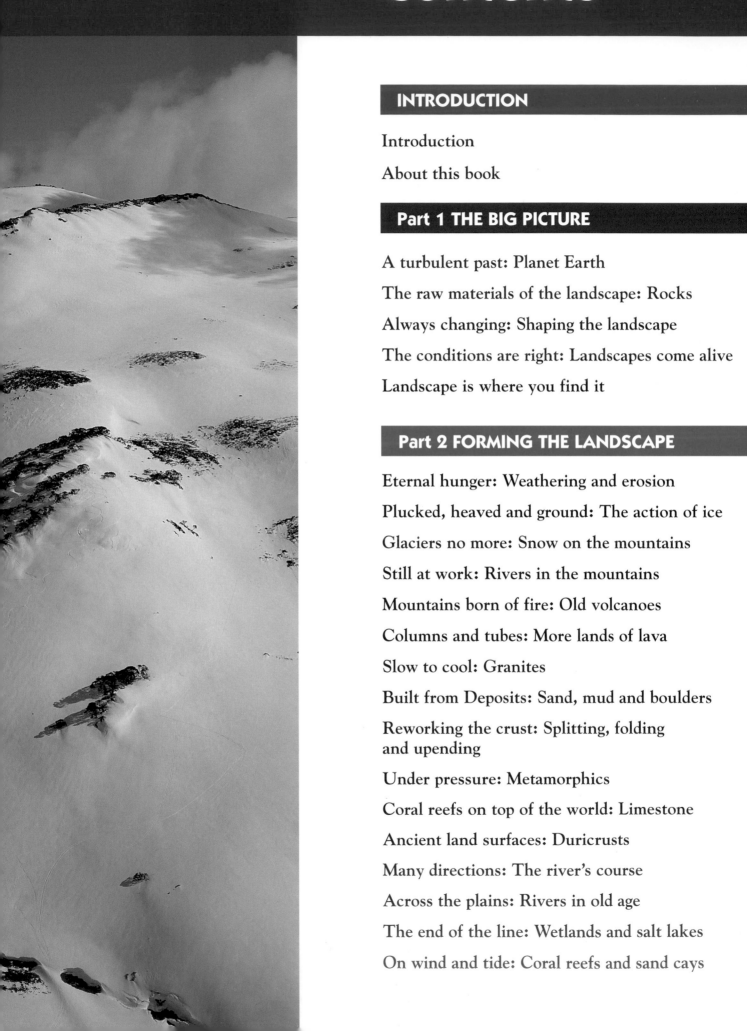

## Part 3 CLASSIC LANDSCAPES

## Part 4 PROTECTING THE LANDSCAPE

# Introduction

**For more than 60,000 years, Aborigines have viewed the landscape and its animals and plants, even the people, as the work of powerful creation beings. They see everything as being related; in a sense, the Australian landscape is a book of stories.**

Europeans, with a different way of viewing the land, arrived on the continent in 1788. Within two years the people were on the brink of starvation. Their knowledge was of a European landscape, where droughts were infrequent and deep, rich, young soils mostly fertile. Naturally, these people had little understanding of the Australian climate, of bushfires, of deserts, of ancient infertile soils, of trees which lost bark and appeared to keep their leaves, or of the weird marsupials. In their ignorance, they wrought vast damage in just two centuries. They were helped by other immigrants – countless rabbits, goats, sheep, donkeys, camels, horses, cattle, water buffaloes and by plants such as blackberries, lantana and Scotch thistle.

The great difference between the Aboriginal culture and Western culture is that the new arrivals treated their landscape as a commodity which could be cut up, sold, mined, and purposely modified.

The landscape of Australia is not a random, accidental jumble of hills and valleys, rivers and coastlines, desert dunes and coral reefs. It is the result of processes acting every minute of the day.

Most dramatic is the weathering and erosion of the sea cliffs by great storm waves, the collapse of cliffs in places like the Blue Mountains, the build-up of dunes at the head of the Great Australian Bight or the changes that take place in river courses during floods.

Weathering and erosion etch out the skeletons of volcanoes, as in the Warrumbungles, or reduce the ancient granites to Devils Marbles or the tors on Mount Kosciusko. In the Kimberley, the rugged coast is sinking, forming an deeply etched maze of fiords and islands of pink quartzite separated by opalescent sea.

200 million year old sandstones of Kennedy Range (WA)

Generated in a cyclone five thousand kilometres away, a wave is finally halted by the coast at Terrigal (NSW)

The Bungle Bungles, striped with orange sandstone and grey limey shale.

rising blisters of magma*, mudflats, coral reefs, heat-hardened sediments, injections of minerals have all been worked on by wind, water, ice, earthquakes, and heat at the surface. The land, responding to these forces, takes on a shape that reflects the nature of the underlying rocks.

To understand the processes of landscape formation is to understand the Earth itself, the only home for humans that we know for sure exists. This book will help to reveal the secrets of the ancient landscapes of Australia.

## About this book

The contents pages will give a good indication of the different landscapes covered in this book. Specialist terms, marked in the text with an asterisk (*) are explained in the Glossary on page 78 the first time they are mentioned. Some further reading is listed on page 79 and a map on the same page shows some of the locations mentioned in the text. An index on the last page of the book will help you to look up topics you are interested in.

In the same place is a vast curving ancient coral reef, now a limestone range cut by stunning gorges of Geikie and Windjana. Deposited on a sea floor, 1600 million years ago, the sandstones of Kakadu have been uplifted and very slow erosion has fretted out the remarkably detailed plateau and escarpment.

Most of us have more questions than answers as we gaze out over the landscape. Volcanoes, massive

# THE AGES OF THE EARTH

| TIME IN MILLIONS OF YEARS | SOME EVENTS | ERA |
|---|---|---|
| 1.6 | | CAINOZOIC |
| 66.4 | Australia solo | CAINOZOIC |
| 144 | First flowers | MESOZOIC |
| 208 | First mammals | MESOZOIC |
| 245 | First reptiles | MESOZOIC |
| 286 | | PALAEOZOIC |
| 360 | First amphibians | PALAEOZOIC |
| 408 | First land plants | PALAEOZOIC |
| 436 | | PALAEOZOIC |
| 505 | | PALAEOZOIC |
| 570 | | PALAEOZOIC |
| 1000 | Multicelled animals | PROTEROZOIC |
| 2000 | Traces of animal life | PROTEROZOIC |
| 3000 | North Pole stromatolites | PROTEROZOIC |
| 4000 | | ARCHAEAN |

A TURBULENT PAST

# Planet Earth

The Sun's heat powers the atmosphere

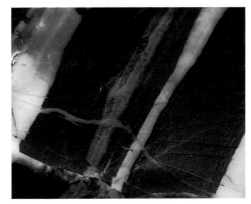
Rock, the raw material of landscape

The water cycle shapes land

# The Earth's formation

**The land surface is constantly being weathered, eroded and transported to other places by wind, water and ice. This devouring of the surface could not continue unless land was also being created.**

The transport of material from one part of the Earth's surface to another place causes the crust to become unstable. Like a see-saw, areas sink under the extra weight while opposite areas, becoming lighter, rise to form mountain ranges.

The hardness of the rock skin is misleading. The crust is only about 50–100 kilometres deep under the continents and much thinner beneath the oceans. The continents are huge rocky rafts known as continental plates*, floating and drifting on a soft, plastic* ocean of hot rock.

From time to time, the continental plates split. Lava oozes out of the split and begins to force the pieces apart. A new ocean basin is born. The split in the centre continuously oozes lava, and the continental pieces are

pushed further and further apart until they collide with other plates. There, the crust is crumpled. Mountains rise and it is there also that the deepest ocean trenches form. These places of collision are also places of earthquakes and of belts of volcanoes, and where minerals are deposited.

Inside the continents too areas are lifted, like the skin over massive blisters, as melted rock is injected from deep below.

The surface of the Earth is constantly on the move, in places being destroyed, in places changed and in other places re-created.

# Australia's origins

Australia is a continental plate on the move northwards, throwing up its northern edge and building the mountains of New Guinea. Much of Australia's surface is very old, with erosion exposing the ancient skeletons of its geology.

This island continent has a recorded geological story dating back nearly 4300 years. The last chapter, which records the split from Antarctica, begins about 55 million years ago. Australia has drifted into the tropics and has felt many climatic changes. Its present-day landscapes are the result of many processes shaping the surface and its edge with the sea. The last million years of change produced today's Australia.

### AUSTRALIA'S DRIFT

50 million years ago          30 million years ago

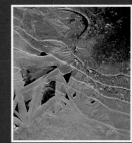
Ice expands and breaks rock

Beating rain mobilises mud

Running water powers erosion

Most rivers deliver salts/silt to the sea

# Rocks

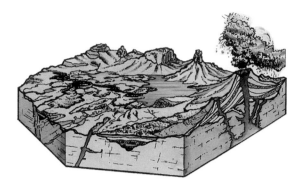

**A VOLCANIC LANDSCAPE**

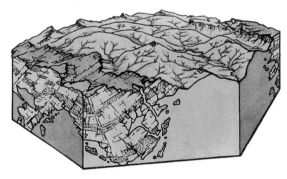

**A GRANITE LANDSCAPE**

## Rocks born of volcanic fire

Probably the first crust on the Earth was of rocks formed by the cooling magma* of volcanoes. These are called igneous rocks*. Even today, 80 per cent of the mass of the crust is igneous. Magma, which is usually 50 to 200 km below the Earth's surface, is forced upwards, like toothpaste from a tube, under the weight of the Earth's crust.

Very hot (900–1200°C) magma is very fluid and breaks through cracks in the land (called rifts) formed by land being pulled apart. The magma floods valleys with layer upon layer of lava forming terraces, plateaus and shield volcanoes*. If the lava cools rapidly, the rock formed will be fine-grained, dense basalt*, dark in colour. Sometimes, during cooling, masses of

hexagonal columns form.

If the lava is less fluid and cooler, the volcanic pipes* become plugged. Under intense pressure, these volcanoes are shattered by explosions. Ash and debris fall like a cone about the cooling core. Erosion of the cone leaves spires of rock, as found at the Warrumbungles in New South Wales.

Cooler magma (600–800°C) frequently rises slowly from deep magma chambers, like vast balloons rising through the crust. Most of these batholiths* cool slowly some 7 km below the surface. Cooling minerals migrate through the thickening magma to become the crystals in granite rocks. Ultimately, erosion removes the covering crust.

The Warrumbungles (NSW), a typical volcanic landscape

Huge boulders are common in granite landscapes

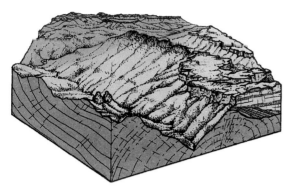

**A SEDIMENTARY LANDSCAPE**

**A METAMORPHIC LANDSCAPE**

## Layers in the landscape

Nowhere on Earth do landscapes remain the same. Plants, animals, the weather, earth movements and gravity are breaking down the land. Ice, water and wind transport the eroded material to the lowlands where it is deposited in a coastal basin or on the ocean floor.

Here, layer upon layer of mud (shale*), sand (sandstone*), gravel, boulders (conglomerate*) and the remains of plants and animals (fossils) are deposited. Sometimes the layers (strata*) are many kilometres thick. The Carnarvon Gorge in Queensland is an example.

Faulting, folding and other massive earth movements uplift these low sediments to become mountain ranges. Then the whole process will start over again – erosion, transport, deposition, uplift.

## Cooked rocks

Metamorphic rocks* are those which have changed under intense pressure and heat. So shale is altered to become slate* or schist* – fine rocks which break in clean sheets. Sandstone becomes more compact and fuses (melts) into a tight mass which is very resistant to erosion. This is quartzite*, frequently seen as massive blocks. When granite is heated to become plastic the mineral crystals tend to gather into bands, becoming gneiss*.

Metamorphism occurs deep beneath the surface where continental plates are colliding, where intense folding is taking place, or in the surroundings of the rising magma of batholiths. A weathered cliff-face, like that at Frome Creek in South Australia, clearly shows many layers of metamorphic rock.

Layered cliffs of sandstone, Carnarvon Gorge (Qld)

Slate cliffs, Frome Creek, Flinders Ranges (SA)

► All of Australia's rivers put together carry only half as much water as the Mississippi River.

► Nearly 90% of water vapour moving through the water cycle evaporates from the ocean.

► About a third of Australia receives less than 200 mm of rain per year. East Lake Eyre (SA) region receives 100 mm of rain per year.

► In tropical Australia granite may rot as deeply as 50 m. Without plant cover, massive erosion takes place.

After a flash flood

ALWAYS CHANGING

# Shaping the landscape

The Earth is always undergoing change. Perhaps it is not as fast as things change around us, but scientists have been able to measure or estimate changes that have taken place over hundreds and thousands of years. Continents move, climates change, there is flood and drought, the oceans rise and fall, volcanoes erupt, rainforests become deserts: all these changes and more are part of Australia's landscape story. These are the big changes, but behind them the land's surface is constantly sculpted by chemical change, water, wind, ice, temperature change and gravity.

Dunes and gullies, Finke (NT)

## Soup from solid rock

Water is the universal solvent (dissolving agent) and is made more effective when it is warm. As rain falls it reacts with carbon dioxide in the air and becomes a weak acid which dissolves limestone. As it runs down the limestone it etches sharp, small gullies in the rock. All rocks have vertical cracks within them, called joints, formed when they cool or shrink. Water seeping down these joints begins to dissolve the rock-faces. Rocks such as granite or basalt are a mixture of minerals. These dissolve at different rates causing the rock to "rot". Even very resistant minerals, such as silica*, will dissolve.

Desert mesas*

Many sedimentary rocks have salts within them when they are formed. When moisture penetrates the salts (and the feldspars* in granites), they swell and physically push flakes and pieces of the surface off. Rock blocks with sharp angles and corners are attacked from two sides and become rounded. This is called spheroidal (rounded) weathering and is best seen on granite and at Uluṟu.

ALLAN FOX

Weathering of sandstone

Red dunes and salt flats in the Simpson Desert

Needle ice, a rock cracker

An old river, The Murray

A young river, Kakadu (NT)

The dissolved salts and sediments from the rotting rocks are washed downhill as the water flows to its lowest level. While the water rushes along its turbulent course from the mountains, the swirling sediment* grinds down gorges and canyons. Leaving the mountains, the river slows and begins to wind (meander) dropping its load of sediment. Flood plains form as the river slowly makes its way to the sea, still carrying dissolved salts. Above, clouds of pure water vapour are being blown inshore to condense and fall as rain across the ranges, keeping the erosion processes active. Salt is left in the ocean.

## Arid landscapes

Apart from the Antarctic, Australia is the driest continent in the world. Many of its landforms are those of deserts and arid areas.

Temperature extremes (from −5 to 45°C), wind, fire, and intense rain all play important roles in creating arid landscapes. They are usually sparsely covered with vegetation. However, there are many plants well adapted to the climatic conditions and, from time to time, the arid country develops a heavy plant cover which dries out, then burns, leaving the ground bare and powdery. Rock surfaces are heated and shattered.

Under these conditions, wind lifts the dust and sand and moves it in willy-willies, or in dust storms. Dunes are built, but in rain storms their surfaces are deeply scoured as the water carries away the sand. Flash floods occur, sweeping all before them until the muddy waters stop running and are swallowed by the wide sandy river beds. The flood plains are the richest wildlife habitats, supporting a great variety of plants and animals.

A model river entering the sea, Thistle Cove, Cape Le Grande (WA)

## FACTS

▶ The Tully area in north Queensland has Australia's highest rainfall: 4300 mm per year.

▶ The major dune systems of the Red Centre formed around 20 000 years ago during the last major Ice Age.

▶ Present sea levels were set 6000 years ago. Today's beaches, frontal dunes* and headlands are no older, though their shaping may have begun during previous high sea levels.

▶ The red colour of the soil in the Red Centre is iron oxide stain.

A turbulent stream

# Landscapes come alive

A tropical environment with great diversity, Litchfield National Park (NT)

Ulysses Butterfly

There are very few places anywhere on Earth where there are dead landscapes. Even the dry valleys in the Antarctic have some simple living things colonising them. From the top of the highest mountains, to the deserts, the sea, or in limestone caves, there is life. All the places photographed in this book are habitats for living things.

How is it that our planet is most likely the only one in our solar system to carry life as we know it?

First, our planet is the right mass. If it were as large as Jupiter, its gravity would hold in an atmosphere so dense that sunlight would not reach the surface and there would be a deadly mix of gases.

Earth is just the right distance from the Sun to provide enough warmth and the planet's tilted axis creates the seasonal climates. Because there is enough warmth, water will stay liquid and dissolve the materials that plants and animals need for life. Water can become a vapour in daytime temperatures and circulate in the water cycle, condensing into rain and then running as streams carrying sand and rubble to shape the land. The ocean water stabilises the temperature

Satin Bower Bird

A wet sclerophyl forest of tall eucalypts and ferns in the Dandenongs (Vic)

Saltwater Crocodile

Crocodile habitat, a mangrove system on the mudflats of Hinchinbrook (Qld)

extremes and, with currents, can shift heat or cold about the planet. Water as ice is a major shaping force.

Of the 100 or so chemical elements which make up the planet, there are 20 which work together in various ways to make plant and animal tissue, to provide energy and food. One of them, carbon, is formed as an atom in such a way that it is able to lock onto many other elements to create plant and animal tissue. Remarkably, sea water contains all of the elements necessary for living organisms.

Some time long ago, simple cells formed (bacteria* and algae*) which thrived under special environmental conditions. At a time when the gas carbon dioxide was very common in the air, some of these cells changed and were able to use the energy of sunlight to link carbon dioxide with water to form sugar and to store the energy. This stored energy could then be used to produce more and more complex cells and groups of cells. The way was then open for an explosion of plant life.

At the same time as carbon was tied into plant matter, oxygen gas was freed to become more and more common in the air. Because plant food and oxygen were available, animal life could develop into the range of species that were ancestors of those we know today.

Kangaroo habitat, Flinders Ranges National Park (SA)

A Euro in the hills

# Landscape is where you find it

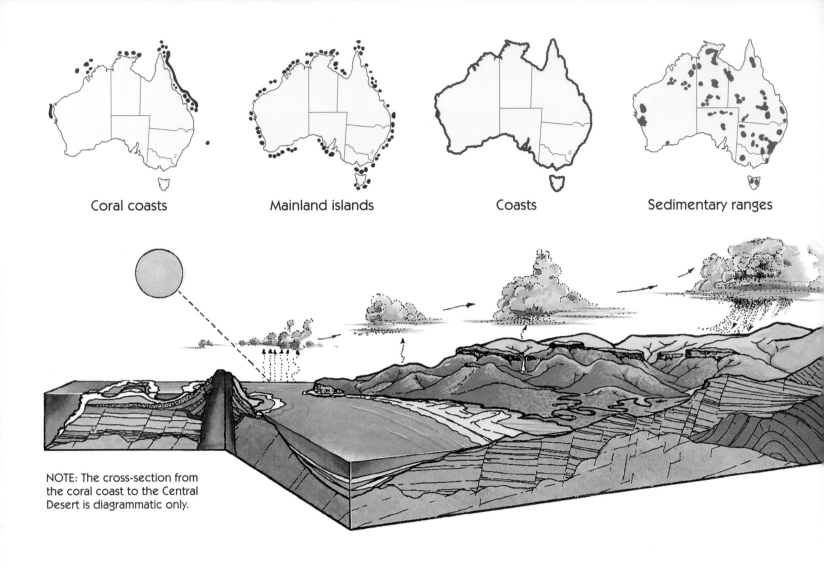

Coral coasts

Mainland islands

Coasts

Sedimentary ranges

NOTE: The cross-section from the coral coast to the Central Desert is diagrammatic only.

1. Coral coasts
Great Barrier Reef (Qld)

2. Mainland islands
Whitsunday Islands (Qld)

3. Coasts
South Head, Sydney (NSW)

4. Sedimentary ranges
Blue Mountains (NSW)

Granite and high tops

Volcanics

Folds, faults and upends

Slopes, downs and plains

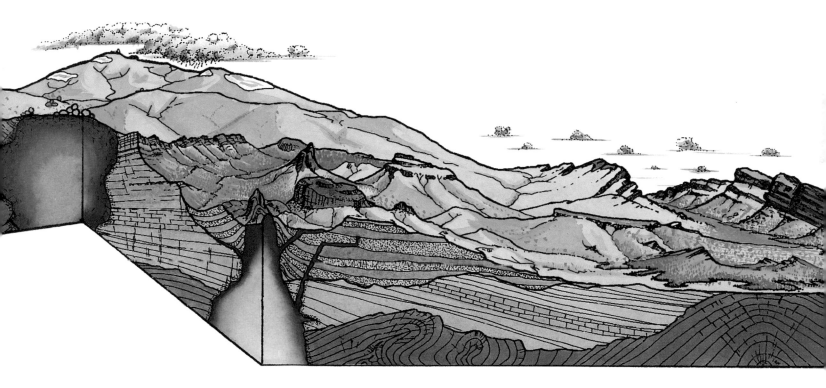

Joins diagram on pages 16 and 17

5. Granite and high tops
   Kosciusko National Park (NSW)

6. Volcanics
   The Warrumbungles (NSW)

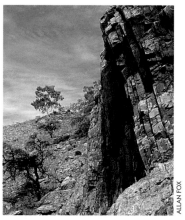

7. Folds, faults, upends
   Petermann Ranges (WA)

8. Slopes, downs and plains
   Northwest plains, Moree (NSW)

# Landscape is where you find it

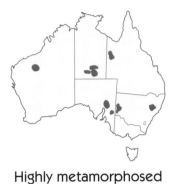

Highly metamorphosed

Senile rivers

Lakes, lunettes and limestones

Astro-craters

Joins diagram on pages 14 and 15

9. Highly metamorphosed
North Flinders Ranges (SA)

10. Senile rivers, wetlands
Barwon River, Walgett (NSW)

11. Lakes, lunettes & limestones
Lake Mungo (NSW)

12. Astro-craters
Gosses Bluff (NT)

Mesas, buttes and pillars

Dunefields

Playas and salt lakes

Domes and hogbacks

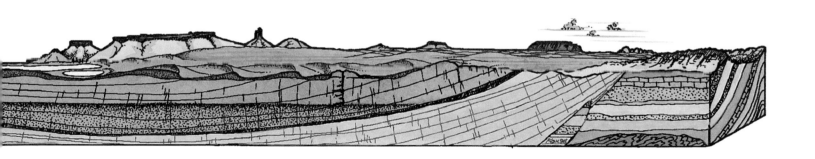

13. Mesas, buttes and pillars
Chambers Pillar (NT)

14. Dunefields
Uluru (NT)

15. Playas and salt lakes
Mt Wedge area (NT)

16. Domes and hogbacks
Waterhouse Range (NT)

## FACTS

▶ The deepest and most rapid weathering occurs in the wet, warm tropical lands.

▶ Sealing the surface of stone does not protect it from weathering, much of which occurs because of the movement of water within the rock.

▶ Plants assist rapid weathering: they produce acids and, as their roots and stems grow, they force open cracks and lift surfaces.

ETERNAL HUNGER

# Weathering and erosion

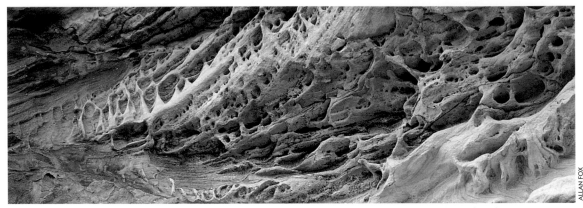

Honeycomb weathering caused by expanding wet salt crystals and wind in Hawkesbury Sandstone

A visit to a cemetery reveals evidence of the effect of weathering on stone. The inscriptions on most memorials are carved into the polished or ground surfaces of one of three main groups of rock: sandstone, marble and granite. Engraving on sandstone loses its sharpness; marble seems to melt along the edges; and the polished granite becomes pitted with holes. The effects of weathering in the cemetery are similar to what takes place in the landscape.

## The bite of mechanical weathering

It is rare to find rock without weaknesses. Usually as molten rock cools, it develops patterns of cracks. The thousands of metres of rock laid down as beds of gravel, sand and mud, or as old sand dunes, are under enormous pressure. The beds split apart and fine cracks run at right angles between the beds. The beds are also of varying strength. Water, which is usually slightly acid, seeps into these cracks and starts to penetrate the rock. If it freezes, the water expands and begins, in small ways, to blow the surface apart.

The erosive impact of water and plants in the Blue Mountains (NSW)

Chemical weathering of limestone, Geikie Gorge (WA)

A cave in weathered sandstone and shale, Anvil Rock

Towers of sandstone isolated by weathering of vertical cracks (joints), Limmen Gate (NT)

Moisture also starts to dissolve minerals and salts in the rock. Heat and dryness on the surface drag up salty moisture. Salt concentrations build up crystals just under the rock's surface. When they are wet, the crystals expand, forcing grains and flakes of rock to fall off. The rock particles are picked up and moved by running water and wind. Where wind and running water are strong, the particles become cutting agents; for example, the stinging dry sand on the beach. Resistant parts of rock remain standing, which causes differential weathering as in the photo below.

## The bite of chemical weathering

Chemical weathering is due to chemicals, usually in rain, reacting with the chemicals in the minerals of the Earth's crust. Water is the most important factor in chemical weathering. It contains the chemicals and it carries away the results of weathering to expose new rock.

Chemical weathering processes are very complex. They are most effective if rock has been broken into small pieces by mechanical weathering.

Differential weathering of sandstone, Kakadu (NT)

Weathering granite, Remarkable Rocks (SA)

# The action of ice

A cirque lake carved into quartzite by glacial action plucking out the rock, Arthur Range (Tas)

Between 286 and 277 million years ago, half of Australia was covered by glaciers. Just south of Adelaide, at Hallett Cove, it is possible to see where that ice, with boulders embedded, ripped deep grooves into the underlying country. Rock faces were polished by ice carrying sand and working like a giant grindstone. A small reserve also protects beautiful cream and pink mounds of rock "flour" created by the grinding glacier. Other remnants of these first Ice Ages are seen as beds of tillite* in Arkaroola Creek and nearby Flinders Ranges.

Glacier flour remains, Hallett Cove, SA

All of Australia's high country was affected by freezing processes between ten and thirty thousand years ago. Today, only Barrington Tops, the Snowy Mountains, the Bogong High Plains and Tasmania are consistently affected by snow and ice.

Needle ice and freeze and thaw* action create many features. Water and moisture in the soil and rock cracks begin to freeze where they are exposed

Needle ice, biting and lifting

Toe of a glacier with moraines, Susten Pass, Austria

Boulders carried by glaciers (erratics), Mt Field (Tas)

to the chilled air. Water expands as it freezes. So it is that countless, needle-like wedges of ice force their way into the soil and into and under rocks. Soil and rocks are moved, both becoming unstable. When it thaws, ice shrinks, becomes water again and with water collecting from melting snow, moves the unstable soil and rocks downhill.

Where there is a long period of freezing, the ice goes deep into the ground.

During the Ice Ages the highlands of Tasmania and a small part of the Snowy Mountains carried glaciers. Ice, like water, seeks to run downhill. Unlike water, it grips the rock it is perched on. Eventually, its weight and the drag of gravity become too great and it tears away, plucking out lumps of rock. Year after year this plucking goes on carving out a deepening and widening dish-like hollow, the cirque. The glacier carries the rock to its melting edge where it is

Glaciated Tasmanian highlands, Arthur Ranges (Tas)

dropped as a moraine, a collection of rocks. The hollows fill with water, forming small mountain lakes called tarns. In Tasmania's southwest, glacial action has produced sharp-peaked alpine skylines.

Glacial lake with moraines, Mt Field National Park (Tas)
ALLAN FOX

## A GLACIER

cirque

snow patch

lateral moraine

erratic

cirque

erratic

glacier

terminal moraine

toe of glacier

# Snow on the mountains

Deep snow on the Main Range, Snowy Mountains

Winter on Mt Feathertop (Vic)

Nowadays, the weather is not cold enough for long enough for the snow to form glaciers and continue shaping the land. In mid-June, however, the first snowfalls can be expected in the Australian Alps, as the weather bringing snow comes in a surge of cold air which sweeps in from the Antarctic.

The thaw begins

From about June, heavy grey clouds come in from the southwest and begin dumping snow on a belt of ranges from Tasmania in a great crescent across Mts Baw Baw, Howitt, Bogong and Buffalo in Victoria, to the high plains, to the Snowy Mountains, and north as far as the New England Tableland in New South Wales. Drifts build up like dunes in the eddying air behind boulders, trees and ridges. When the storm is over, lower snows thaw quickly but the colder high plains and ranges hold their snows, building the cover with each storm until they are smooth and white under a silencing blanket, in places metres deep.

Snowy Mountains in November

# Rivers in the mountains

Coomera River, McPherson Range (Qld) of volcanic rock; a rich footing for plants and the head for many rivers

▶ Australian tropical streams usually flood during December to March and, after June, they have little or no flow.

▶ Mountain tropical streams, such as the Mosman in north Queensland, carry heavy bed loads* of boulders causing great turbulence and scouring of river banks and bed.

▶ Plunge pools are formed by erosion at the foot of a waterfall.

▶ The collapse of bubbles in turbulent water causes strong shock waves to hammer the bed and banks of the stream.

▶ Mountain streams sometimes cut back into the headwaters of another river. This is called river piracy.

▶ Water in the plunge pool below an active waterfall has much air mixed with it reducing its buoyancy capacity (i.e. swimmers sink).

## Tropical river landscapes

**Across tropical northern Australia, the upland streams come to life in the wet season and the erosion of the landscape continues.**

December brings in the monsoonal wet, first with violent storms then the true monsoon during which steady heavy rain falls each day. On the sandstone plateau of Kakadu the stone, dehydrated during the intense heat of the dry, absorbs its fill. First it leaks, then it sheds the rain as it falls.

The sandstone is old and crazed with many joints. This network fills and runs, carrying abrasive sand. Network joins network, channels widen and merge. They become a leaping stream, dashing over steps as strata break away. Plunge pools boil below as the water cascades over the edge of the plateau and sand, pebbles and boulders act as cutting tools. At Jim Jim Falls, there are two steps dropping 200 m and the head of the gorge is misted with spray.

The brink, Jim Jim Falls

Jim Jim Falls falling

Jim Jim Falls plunge pool

Turbulent Jim Jim Creek in the gorge

On the way to the plains

# Old volcanoes

The Glasshouse Mountains (Qld), 25 million years old. Each plug* is the core of a volcano

## FACTS

▶ A sill is a body of volcanic rock formed when magma forces its way between two layers of sedimentary rock.

▶ Millions of years ago, the Warrumbungle Volcano changed the course of the Castlereagh River (NSW) which now almost encircles the ranges.

▶ The most recent volcanic action in Australia was in western Victoria where the average eruption period was 13 000 years ago.

**Australia has no active volcanoes today, but the Glasshouse and Warrumbungle mountains and Mt Warning are the remaining cores of old volcanoes.**

For about 45 million years Australia has been drifting northwards across the asthenosphere*. About 33 million years ago the continent began passing over hotspots, which are deep upwellings of magma. The hot, fluid magma, under tremendous pressure, broke through weaknesses in the Earth's crust at various places. Over the next 27 million years, some 30 central volcanoes erupted over these hotspots. The last was the Macedon Volcano, six million years ago.

Dyke*: an injection of basalt

Lord Howe Island: the remains of a huge undersea volcano

Volcanic plugs: Crater Bluff and Tonduron

The Warrumbungle (NSW) volcano was 45 km wide

Mt Warning, centre of the Tweed Volcano

Breadknife, Warrumbungles, cast of a dyke

Very old volcanoes once broke through the Sydney sandstone region. They are now deep, usually circular hollows, called necks, with rich soil in the bottom.

The largest was the huge Tweed Volcano. Mt Warning is the central plug, a mass of solidified lava, which once filled the central vent of the volcano, and which has been exposed by weathering. The mountains in the Warrumbungle group are the remains of a triple central volcano, 15–18 million years old. There was a line of volcanoes running from near Kingaroy in Queensland to Orange and Oberon in New South Wales.

This 800 kilometre chain began with minor volcanic activity and increased to a point where the magma began to melt the rock deep down. It then became a major volcano until the pressure and supply of magma declined and activity diminished.

When a volcano dies, wind and rain erosion etch out the less resistant ash, rubble and sandy tuffs*. The volcanic plugs are left standing as spires, dykes as walls, flows of lava as tablelands and plains, and piled layers of volcanic debris as great sugarloaf (cone-shaped) mountains. Australia has little evidence of the presence of towering explosive volcanoes (strato-volcanoes) in its history.

Mt Tongariro, New Zealand, is a strato-volcano

25

## FACTS

▶ A maar is a volcanic crater, often a lake, surrounded by a low circle of material thrown up as hot lava explodes on contact with water.

▶ Scoria are fragments of volcanic lava which were formed during violent eruptions.

▶ When lava fills old river beds and valleys, later erosion frequently carves away the valley sides leaving the lava as a ridge top. Beneath the lava the old river bed can be dug out along with gold and other minerals. This is called a deep lead.

▶ Fine fossils of plants, fish and birds have been found in beds of diatomaceous* earth formed in hot spring lagoons of the Warrumbungle Volcano.

COLUMNS AND TUBES

# More lands of lava

Ebor Falls (NSW) plunging over the edge of an old volcanic flow

Sawn Rocks, Mt Kaputar NP (NSW)

There are many sites with reminders of a fiery past. Sawn Rocks in Mt Kaputar National Park is a classic example of hexagonal rock columns formed by volcanic action. The Undara Lava Tubes in north Queensland were formed 190 000 years ago. One extends 160 km to the Einasleigh River, another 90 km to the Lynd River.

Hot, fluid lava poured from great splits or rifts in the Earth's crust, or injected between vertical layers within the crust, forming layers of basalt. Cooling centres formed on the surface and, as cooling continued, cracks ran inwards from these centres. As at Sawn Rocks, columns formed separated from the adjoining centres by fine cracks.

Crater lake, Lake Eacham (Qld)

Mt Hay, Leura (NSW), capped with basalt

Landscape of terraced basalt flows, Merriwa (NSW)

A basalt flow from Tweed Volcano weathered to hexagonal columns, Fingal Head (NSW)

Lava flows like honey and when it runs into a valley it follows the valley. The surface hardens but the lava keeps flowing beneath the surface. These are lava tubes. Some of the world's longest are at Undara, northwest of Townsville in Queensland. The amount of lava released from rifts in the hard surface can frequently be measured in many cubic kilometres. Layer upon layer runs out until vast areas are covered by terraced plains of lava. This may be seen north from Merriwa in New South Wales. Parts of the Blue Mountains were covered with lava flows and today some of this cap is seen covering Mts Hay and Tomah.

In Tasmania much of the Central Highlands down to the Hartz Mountains, Mt Wellington and Capes Raoul and Pillar are of volcanic dolerite* which was injected as a vast sill 300–500 m thick into ancient Tasmania's structure. About 160 million years of erosion has exposed the resistant dolerite now on top.

Eastern Australia is littered with volcanic sites.

Peaks of resistant dolerite, Cradle Mountain, Lake St Claire National Park (Tas)

A collapsed section of Undara lava tubes

# Granites

The Devils Marbles (NT), piles of granite tors encircled by hills which once covered the granite

## FACTS

▶ Liquid magma may rise from deep below the crust or may be molten rock from the collision of drifting continents when one of the plates is forced a hundred or so kilometres below the other.

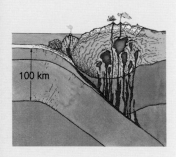

100 km

▶ Granites have clear, large crystals of glassy silica, shiny clear to black mica flakes and white, cream to pink blocks of feldspar.

▶ The edges of granite fields are frequently shot through with veins of milky quartz and other minerals.

▶ Rising magma brings to the surface gaseous matter such as steam. Much of the ocean waters have collected over billions of years from this source.

Large amounts of rising molten rock do not reach the surface but instead begin to slowly cool and harden kilometres under the Earth's surface. This forms a batholith, a large body of igneous rock, shaped like a great hot-air balloon. For millions of years they cool and during this time the three main kinds of minerals of granite (silica, mica and feldspar) collect into crystals. Silica is glass-like. The colour of granite comes from the mix that makes the mica and the feldspar.

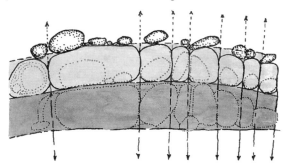

As granite cools, small deep cracks (the joints) form. Weathering processes eat out these cracks forming round blocks (the tors).

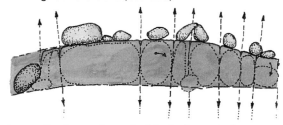

Layer after layer of granite blocks is eroded away

Formation of tors at Devils Marbles (NT)

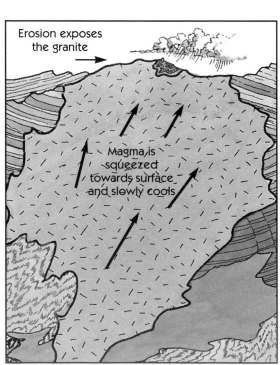

Erosion exposes the granite

Magma is squeezed towards surface and slowly cools

**FORMATION OF A GRANITE BATHOLITH**

Exfoliation* at work

Smooth rounded slopes and exfoliation on the mountain top, Bald Rock (NSW)

Granite seascape, Thistle Cove (WA)

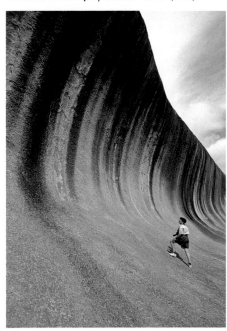
Wave Rock, Hyden (WA), formed when soil was 11 m higher – the rock was rotted by the damp soil

While a batholith is cooling, vapours and solutions of rare minerals that do not fit into the crystal structure of the three main components leak into surrounding rock. Minerals such as gold, silver, copper, lead and zinc fill cracks and rifts caused by the rising batholith, becoming veins or massive ore bodies.

Kilometres above, as the surface is constantly eroded, the land mass rises. After perhaps 50 or 100 million years, the crown of the batholith appears on the surface. In some places where the Earth's crust is under pressure, it begins to fault and fold, and the granite mass is uplifted.

Weathering and erosion penetrate joints isolating some of the layers of huge blocks. These are then rounded off by weathering to stand as tors. In some places, whole mountains are rounded to gigantic tors because of the uniform mix of crystals in the granite. At the Devils Marbles in the Northern Territory, the typical weathering of granite is very clear. At these places the tors appear to be losing successive skins, like onions. This process is called exfoliation.

There are many "wave rocks" in granite landscapes. It appears that weathering occurred when the rock was underground. Water runs off the hill keeping the soil wet at depth. The waves are usually on the southern sides of hills where evaporation is less.

BUILT FROM DEPOSITS

# Sand, mud & boulders

Sheer massive sandstone cliffs collapsing because of undermining, Kennedy Ranges (WA)

By looking closely at a landscape, it is possible to "read" its layers to tell its geological history. Above the forest-covered coal-bearing slopes of Mt Banks in the Blue Mountains, golden sandstone cliffs climb 400 m to the capping of dark volcanic rock. Here, layer upon layer, like the pages of a book, lies the story of the past.

Collapse of Blue Mountain cliffs, Govetts Leap (NSW)

At the bottom are 250 million-year-old coal and shale seams. The golden sandstones took about 10 million years to be deposited in the shallows of the Sydney Basin. Then, in swamps and lagoons on the old river plains, layers of river mud settled and later became shales. All of this country was slowly uplifted allowing weathering and erosion to shape the landscape.

## The land is never still

While weathering and erosion were shaping the Blue Mountains and all of the sandstone which may have held most of the dinosaur fossils was removed, other sandstones were being formed to the north. About 210 million years ago, a river network flowed eastwards from western Queensland across a conifer-covered landscape. Clean white sands were carried and then deposited along with

Rivers roll and grind boulders

Boulder stream

Reduction in size to gravel

30

Sheets of mudstone, Kalbarri, Western Australia

conifer logs to form the white sandstones of Carnarvon Gorge in Queensland. These are appropriately named Precipice Sandstones. The dark brown holes in the sandstone are fossil logs.

This process of weathering, erosion, transport, deposition and uplift, has always taken place. For instance, the sandstones of the Arnhem Plateau in Kakadu are extremely ancient and still lie flat. For 1600 million years weathering and erosion have carved the most intricate images in the landscape. Now thousands of massive blocks, creating hundreds of caverns, balance precariously. Sand and mud from the now empty caverns and eroding slopes have been carried by creeks and rivers fed by countless wet seasons to be deposited in the swamps and on the sea bed.

Uluru and Kata Tjuta, 300 million years ago, were being uplifted and folded as parts of great mountain ranges. In perhaps another 10 million years, even these will be reduced to layers of sand awaiting rebirth in the eternal processes of mountain building.

CYCLE OF EROSION

DEPOSITION > UPLIFT & MOUNTAIN FORMATION v WEATHERING & EROSION & TRANSPORT > DEPOSITION

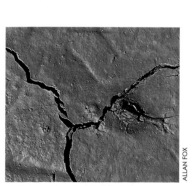
A future fossil shield shrimp

Fossil shells of an old sea

Uplifted sandstone

## FACTS

▶ Sandstone is also formed from wind-blown sand. As it weathers, the old slopes of the dunes are etched out and the form of the dunes can be seen in the stone.

▶ Rocks uplifted in level strata with varying thickness are likely to produce tableland landscapes; rivers cutting them will probably have walled gorges or canyons.

▶ Coarse sandstones act as water filters.

▶ Glaciers with boulders embedded grind deep U-shaped valleys and push masses of rocks and finely ground rock ("flour") into steep ridges. The flour washes into lakes and swamps settling to form the finest sedimentary rock.

▶ Sandstone with pebbles set in it is conglomerate.

▶ Most of the rock-making minerals in the Earth's crust occur in sands.

▶ Quartz is the most common mineral in sand.

The cycle of erosion works world wide: the Grand Canyon, USA

# Splitting, folding and upending

Enormous pressures produce fracturing

ALLAN FOX

Under heat and pressure rock becomes plastic

ALLAN FOX

The Central Australian ranges around Alice Springs were originally deposited in the Amadeus Basin as pebbly sand, fine sand and mud. In the centre of the basin this sediment was about seven kilometres deep around 300 million years ago. Then slow but extremely strong pressures began to work on the basin. Edges buckled and folded.

In parts the strata were crushed, with huge sections breaking and sliding over the breaks. The sandstone of Uluṟu is a good example of this. About 300 million years ago, massive sandstones were put under pressure and they folded. Today, Uluṟu is just a small part of this fold. It stands up at 80° from the horizontal.

## FOLDS AND FAULTS

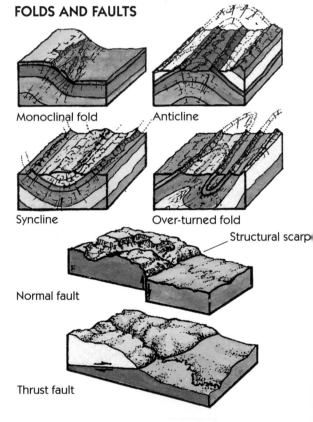

Monoclinal fold

Anticline

Syncline

Over-turned fold

Structural scarp

Normal fault

Thrust fault

An example of a synclinal fold in quartzites, Wilpena Pound, Flinders Ranges (SA)

Totally upended sandstones, Finke River at Glen Helen (NT)

A vast arching fold developed west of Alice Springs. The stretched rock on top of the arch was weakened and broken. Weathering took place rapidly and erosion has taken out the centre of the fold. Only the sides of the fold remain rising from the plain as two mountain ranges (Chewings and Heavitree Ranges).

At Glen Helen, to the west, the ridges run in long parallel lines of grey limestones, orange and red sandstones, sharp purplish shale and a massive ridge of rusty resistant quartzite. All on their edges, they are parts of a vast fold.

Wilpena Pound in the Flinders Ranges in South Australia is the best example in Australia of the way tremendous pressure can bend rock. The quartzite has bent to form a vast saucer – a hollow or "pound" – encircled by rising ranges. This unique geological formation is an example of what is known as a syncline, a trough or a fold in rock strata.

Dipping quartzites, Frome River, Flinders Ranges (SA)

One limb of an anticlinal fold, James Ranges (NT)

## FACTS

▶ Folding and uplifting usually result from a series of very slow movements taking place over millions of years.

▶ The San Andreas Fault in California is moving at an average rate of 4 cm per year.

▶ Most of the mountain building processes are generated by the drifting and colliding of continental plates.

▶ The uplift of the central ranges was so slow that rivers were able to cut their winding channels straight through very resistant quartzite without changing their courses. Faster uplifting would have caused the river to change course.

▶ Folding of rock strata sometimes results in domes of resistant rock which trap rising petroleum gas and oil formed by the breakdown of organic matter deeper down.

▶ All rocks have vertical cracks that don't slip, called joints, formed when they cool or shrink.

Joint in sandstone

33

# Metamorphics

Jasper outcropping to form a bar across the river at Marble Bar (WA)

The white quartzite spine of Frenchman's Cap in western Tasmania and the red and white banded jasper of Marble Bar in Western Australia are in very different climate zones, but they have a common heritage. They were buried and compressed, suffered some melt-down, then they were stirred, and brought to the surface greatly changed.

## Buried and compressed

Most profound changes take place many kilometres into the roots of mountain ranges. Here, with the vast weight of the mountains and the crust pressing down, and with the heat flowing up from below, the rocks become plastic or pliable. Minerals begin to reconstruct themselves and to move in the direction of least pressure, giving many metamorphic rocks a streaming pattern.

A peak of quartzite and schist, Federation Peak (Tas)

Folded quartzites, King Leopold Range (WA)

Highly metamorphosed quartzites and schists, Fitzgerald River National Park (WA)

## Collisions and the big squeeze

When a continental plate of crust is forced against another plate, enormous pressures develop, crumpling the contact area. Temperature rises due to friction. Some of the softened and crumpled rock is squeezed below the oncoming plate, getting hotter the deeper it plunges. In the whole buckled and heated zone, changes (metamorphism) take place. Grains fuse and the rocks become more dense and usually more resistant to later erosion.

Some time later, the metamorphic rocks reach the surface, as erosion or uplift occurs. Their resistant strata form high peaks and barriers to river systems, and are often rich in minerals.

Jasper at Marble Bar (WA)

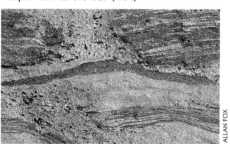

Minerals streaming out, forming gneiss

Slates at Milparinka (NSW)

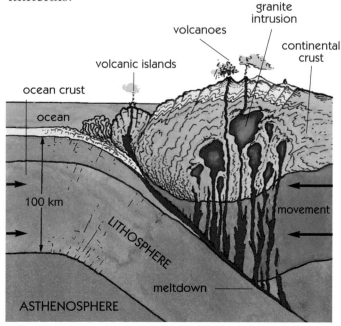

**CONTINENTAL AND OCEANIC PLATES COLLIDE**

ocean crust
ocean
100 km
LITHOSPHERE
meltdown
ASTHENOSPHERE
volcanic islands
volcanoes
granite intrusion
continental crust
movement

# Limestone

Lennard River cutting Windjana Gorge through the Napier Range (WA), an ancient coral reef

**Windjana Gorge, cut by the Lennard River in Western Australia, is a place where reef fish once swam.**

Corals had their origins about 1000 million years ago. Along with molluscs and some algae, they are able to construct, with trillions of their skeletons and shells, massive ranges of limestone. Windjana Gorge cuts through such a reef that was alive 360 million years ago. Since then the land has uplifted about 500 km of this reef to form the Napier Range.

Like most limestone areas this range is criss-crossed with joints down which rain has drained and dissolved the limestone. At varying levels this water ran horizontally along the bedding, eroding cave systems. The walls of the gorge are etched into fluted columns with sharp tops and in places cut by deep rifts and rounded caverns where water once ran. A perfect cross-section of a coral reef can be seen in the walls.

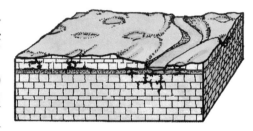

Early stage – high water table

Lowering water table

sink hole    canyon
caves

**EVOLUTION OF A CAVE SYSTEM**

A cavern formed by weathering

A stalactite with calcite drip

Stalagmites

A roof collapse of a giant cave, Bungonia Gorge (NSW)

Limestone cliffs, Napier Range (WA)

Limestone cliffs, Great Australian Bight

At Tunnel Creek, WA, the stream has cut a cavern right through the range. Side caves at various levels up the walls show earlier stream courses. About half way through the cavern, light penetrates the darkness where a hill has fallen in after chemical weathering ate out the joints and released a mass of blocks. This is a sink hole, typical of limestone country. Whole cave systems sometimes collapse forming huge gorges like that at Bungonia in New South Wales.

Caves are an important habitat for many animals, including the Ghost Bat, which cannot survive without caves. When limestone is mined for the making of cement, caves can be destroyed. Sometimes industry and conservation interests are at odds and careful planning and assessment of the environmental effects of mining are needed.

Chemical erosion by a river, Geikie Gorge (NT)

The Grand Arch, Jenolan Caves (NSW)

Typical chemical weathering

## FACTS

▶ Important animal fossils are found where rivers carrying carcasses dump them with mud in limestone caves. Fossil remains found include Tasmanian Tigers, Dingos, possums, Mountain Pygmy Possums, and the earliest evidence of humans in Tasmania.

▶ A sink hole is a depression formed by the collapse of rock above an underground cavern.

▶ Limestone caves are the most important habitat for many bat species and some very unusual invertebrates*.

▶ A Karst region is one in which nearly all the drainage is by underground channels leaving the surface dry and barren.

▶ The Nullarbor Plain is treeless because the limestone country is so dry.

▶ In southeast Asia, China and Yugoslavia large areas of limestone have been eroded along joints to produce a remarkable landscape known as Tower Karst.

Tower Karst, Vietnam

# Duricrusts

Duricrusted caps protect mesas from erosion, Edgar Ranges, Great Sandy Desert (WA)

**Silcrete tablelands of mesas and gibber plains are the most characteristic landscapes of the border country of New South Wales, Queensland and South Australia.**

Silcrete, ferricrete and calcrete are a group of rocks known as duricrust, a durable crust which caps plateaus, tablelands and mesas. Their names give a clue to what the "cement" is which binds the rock: silcrete is cemented by silica, ferricrete by iron oxide and calcrete by calcium carbonate.

### FORMATION OF A DURICRUST

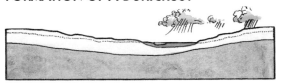

STAGE 1 Saturation and movement of minerals

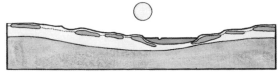

STAGE 2 Minerals form lumps about the water table

STAGE 3 Erosion begins to remove the softer surface

STAGE 4 Hard duricrust caps and protects

The formation of duricrusts goes back about 60 million years when the surface of Australia was even more level than it is today. The continent was just beginning to break from Gondwana and lay between 25 and 60°S. The climate was much wetter. The surface was wet deep down and it is suggested that acid rain was falling, a result of widespread volcanic activity world wide. These conditions produced deep weathering of underlying rock. The deeply weathered rocks at or just below the water table were saturated with water.

The iron-hardened cap of Chambers Pillar (NT)

Streaming white clay: symbol of duricrusts above

Broken down silcrete pebbles, Sturt's Stony Desert

Groundwater, percolating down from the surface, dissolved iron, silica and other elements, moving them down to the saturated, deeply weathered rocks at and just below the water table. The solutions then slowly drained away via springs and seepage. In the draining zone, chemical reactions took place. Concentrated silica (as a gel) combined with iron to form deep red lumps or nodules in the water table region.

Dissolved iron and silica that drained away became concentrated in low-lying areas where these elements filled all of the tiny spaces between the grains in soil or rock. As erosion reduced the landscape, these once-lower but toughened rock areas became the caps protecting table-lands. The gibbers of the stony deserts are all that remains of completely eroded silcrete coverings.

Opals appear to be 30 million years old and formed when special climatic and silcrete processes were operating around the edge of the Great Artesian Basin.

Bauxite capping, part of Cape York (Qld)

Ferricrete capping, Halls Creek (WA)

ALLAN FOX

## FACTS

▶ Weipa is the largest single occurrence of bauxite in the world.

▶ The process by which ferricrete is produced over an iron-rich rock base, results in about a metre of ferricrete in 10 000 years.

▶ Desert varnish is the shiny purple and red coatings of various oxides, particularly iron, which stain the desert pebbles.

▶ Many of the minerals, such as phosphorus, needed by plants are locked up in duricrusts and are unavailable to plants, leaving the countryside bare of vegetation.

▶ Precious opal consists of patterns of micro-scopic spheres of silica.

▶ Groundwater in the Great Artesian Basin extends to a depth of 3000 m where the processes of duricrusting are happening now.

▶ Hollows and caves run deep under the duricrusted caps and provide shelter for Hill Kangaroos.

▶ Silcrete was quarried by Aborigines to provide fine, sharp-edged tools.

# The river's course

The Katherine River (NT) has its course set by joints and faults

**Rock type (e.g., sandstone, granite), rock structure (e.g., joints, faults, bedding), stage of river development, its volume and speed all affect the river patterns.**

From the air, the hard sandstone plateau of the headwaters of the Katherine River is split into a chessboard pattern of joints and faults.

Millions of wet seasons have carved out a deep, walled gorge which zig-zags its way to the plains. Each straight section carries a long deep pool. At intervals, lesser creeks drop from the side walls. Like the fantastic red gorges of the Hamersleys or those of the East Alligator River, the Katherine River's course is controlled by joints and faults.

In mountainous country where the rocks are of the same kind, such as granites, fine shales or fine

Joffre Gorge, Hamersley Range (WA)

Boulders, tools of erosion

The work of the cutting tools, Carnarvon Creek

Deep waters caused by concentration of flood water scouring out the bed, Lawn Hill Gorge (Qld)

metamorphic rocks, water run-off cuts patterns similar to the branching of a tree: runnels (twigs) join to become gullies (branchlets); gullies join to become creeks (branches); and creeks join to become rivers (trunks). These are called dendritic (tree-like) patterns. Resistant rocky barriers either divert a river or the river ultimately cuts a narrow, cascading channel through it.

Balances in the crust are upset by rivers levelling mountain regions or by the collision of drifting continents causing areas to be uplifted. If this drift is slow, old rivers regain some of their energy and cut their beds deeper. Old rivers stamp their mark on new landscapes.

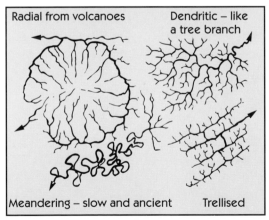

Fault controlled Wollomombi Gorge (NSW)

ALLAN FOX

Radial from volcanoes

Dendritic – like a tree branch

Meandering – slow and ancient

Trellised

**THE PATTERN OF RIVERS**

Entrenched old river patterns, (left) Trephina Gorge and (centre) Ormiston Gorge (NT)          Entrenched channel,   Finke River (NT)

41

# Rivers in old age

An ancient river course across the western plains of New South Wales

**As river systems grow old they tend to level the land, lose their speed and meander, swinging back and forth in a wide, looping course. Old river courses are often given new life by an uplift of the land and rivers of the plains can become rivers of the mountains.**

Because so many rivers across the Great Divide headed off in a northwesterly direction and appeared to become lost in marshes, early explorers looked for an inland sea. John Oxley started the myth in 1816 when his party, following the Lachlan River, were forced to travel along the natural levees* of the river. Away to the south and north great marshes steadily closed in. These were the backswamps* and billabongs of the old river. In the following year he decided to follow the Macquarie River, only to be blocked once again by the river breaking up into many channels which lost themselves in the Macquarie Marshes. Thomas Mitchell and Charles Sturt ultimately proved that these and other rivers were gathered by the Darling and drained into the Murray.

These rivers began collecting the drainage from the rising eastern ranges some 90 million years ago. Ten million years before that, the last of the large inland seas were pushed out by a rising crust and by being filled with sediment.

A meander and cutoff

A senile river, The Bland (NSW)

A billabong lined with River Red Gums

From the highlands, vigorous young streams carried sediment west and south to lowlands and onto a vast sedimentary plain. Here they began to wander. In floods many of the bends or meanders were cut leaving loops isolated when the flood subsided. These are called billabongs. Much silt and mud were pushed up onto the river banks; these became the natural levees.

During periods of higher rainfall, some streams left the main channel totally and made their own way to the Murray or Darling. One of these, the Willandra Creek, has not reached the Murray now for 14 000 years. In the rare flood years it still pours some waters into the first lakes of the Willandra chain. The vast sedimentary plains of inland New South Wales, Queensland and Victoria are overlapping deltas. They have, however, been deposited where there were once shallow seas. Salt now rises to the surface and inhibits plant growth.

The lower Murray, South Australia

The Channel Country, southwest Qld

Rising salt is a threat at Lake Cowal (NSW)

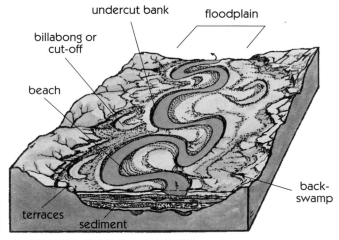

**A MEANDERING SENILE RIVER**

undercut bank

floodplain

billabong or cut-off

beach

back-swamp

terraces

sediment

ALLAN FOX

**FACTS**

▶ Because of the great age of the Murray-Darling system, plants, fish and wildlife are very closely adapted to the natural conditions. Human interference has had serious effects on them.

▶ Clearance of native vegetation in the Victorian Mallee is expected to increase the flow of saline groundwater into the Murray River eight-fold.

▶ The Murray-Darling catchment* covers 1/7 of Australia.

▶ There are many "hidden" channels filled with sand and gravel beneath the surface of the river plains. Many of these hold large volumes of underground water.

▶ The recent construction of dams and ground tanks on the headwaters of the old river systems starved the rivers of fresh flowing water to clear their systems. Blue-green algae grow best in warm, slow moving water polluted with fertilisers.

▶ Human land-use is causing the salinisation of the river plains. As native vegetation, which helped stabilise the water table, is cleared, the water table rises, bringing salt from underground to the surface.

# Wetlands and salt lakes

A seasonal wetland or outwash of the Willandra Creek (NSW)

## DID YOU KNOW?

### FACTS

▶ The water supply for Uluru Resort is pumped from a palaeo-river* 12–20 m down. The water is 7000 years old.

▶ In New South Wales, people drained or filled in 60% of the coastal swamps in one five year period in the 1960s.

▶ Floodouts from desert mountains are places where water and nutrients, washed from the mountains, collect. They are a kind of dry, rich swamp.

▶ Swamps are places rich in nutrients. They are highly susceptible to the effects of human habitation.

▶ The salt crust of a salina* always remains damp with deep greasy mud beneath it.

▶ Land surrounding salinas becomes puffed up with salt and is easily blown away.

## Wetlands

**Swamp landforms may last relatively briefly: they start as lagoons or lakes, slowly fill with sediment and vegetation and are swamps for a short time before filling to become plains.**

In times of flood, major rivers in the Murray-Darling system lose themselves in floodouts when the rivers break their banks. Cut-offs or billabongs are inundated every few years by major floods and many smaller freshes (a rise in a stream due to heavy rains or the melting of snow or ice).

These wetlands release the water slowly, keeping the lower streams running later in the season. However, they have been

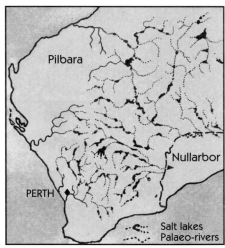

**THE PALAEO-RIVERS OF WESTERN AUSTRALIA**

seriously disrupted by dam building and pastoralism. They were winter to early summer wetlands and their location makes them susceptible to drought.

The wetlands from Townsville in Queensland to Derby in Western Australia can be massive in summer when the monsoons arrive or when cyclones drift inland to drench the country. Huge areas lie submerged for months on end. This is the time when geese, barramundi and prawns build their populations.

Where the Lachlan River becomes the Lowbidgee Marsh (NSW)

Townsville Common (Qld) is a classic tropical coastal swamp which harbours many waterbirds

## Salt lakes and lagoons

In some inland waters the salt level is very high. Here salt has leached from surrounding soils and has been concentrated by evaporation. These are the vast white salt flats and lakes, many in river systems by far the oldest in the country. Eyre, Mackay, Amadeus, Disappointment, Frome, Torrens, Gairdner, Gillies, Everard, Serpentine, Gregory are just some among a thousand or more lakes which hold water for a short time only.

Many mark the sinuous courses of rivers, the palaeo-rivers, ten and more million years old. Such salt lakes are the sign of an ancient land surface. On very rare occasions they hold water on the surface, but usually there is much underground.

ALLAN FOX

A salt lake near Mt Wedge (NT)

The Channel Country after receding flood

Claypans hold shallow water after rain to form a playa, Rainbow Valley (NT)

## FACTS

▶ Water runs from the mountains, slows down in the lowlands and in desert areas evaporates, leaving behind any minerals, including salt, it was carrying. These accumulate in depressions which become salinas or playas*.

▶ The bed of Lake Eyre is 16 m below sea level and receives water from a 1 300 000 km² catchment. Salt and gypsum* crusts and crystals have been brought in by drainage and left by evaporation of the water.

▶ Swamps and wetlands are seriously endangered by drainage, solid waste disposal and chemical pollution. They are essential breeding and feeding areas for many birds and animals, and the nurseries for water-tolerant plants.

# Coral reefs and sand cays

Lady Elliott Island (Qld) on a broad patch reef in the Capricorn Group

Nine thousand years ago, after the last Ice Age, the rising tropical sea began to cover the remains of ancient coral reefs on Queensland's continental shelf*. Clear, warm, sunlit seas swept in the eggs and larvae* of marine life including those of colonising corals. These found the environment ideal and grew vigorously, forming a myriad of reefs. As corals died, their limey skeletons were used as the foundation for new colonisers.

Corals are tiny nocturnal animals, polyps*, which begin life as eggs liberated in countless numbers into the sea across the reef on only a few nights each year. Those that survive become free swimming planula* which attach themselves to a hard surface. Within a day or so these larvae develop a central mouth around which small tentacles grow. A six-section internal skeleton of corallite* stiffens the soft tubular body.

Living inside this body is a small algal plant. These algae are plants which use the energy of the Sun to build sugary food from water and carbon dioxide. As they do this,

A coral rubble spit

Coral polyps at night

A fringing reef

**SAND CAY AND REEF**

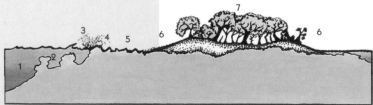

1. BOMMY 2. TRENCH 3. RIM OR REEF CREST 4. CORAL ZONE 5. SAND FLAT 6. BEACH 7. CAY

**PLATFORM REEF**

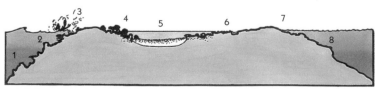

1. REEF SLOPE 2. REEF FRONT 3. ALGAL RIM CREST 4. CORAL FLAT 5. SAND FLAT 6. CORAL FLAT 7. ALGAL RIM 8. REEF BACK

Lady Musgrave Island (Qld), a coral cay

they help the polyp to extract calcium from the water and to build the corallite. They also provide the animal with some of its food. It is thought that the plant is rewarded for this work in carbon dioxide, nitrates and phosphates given off by the polyp.

## Sand cays

Masses of coral rubble torn off the reefs by storms are thrown onto the reef flats. Tides and currents roll the shingle about, gradually breaking it down to sand, a process greatly aided by Wrasse, Parrot Fish and sea cucumbers in their search for food.

Southeast tradewinds drive currents and waves across the sandy and rubbly flat, building a spit, a narrow stretch of land, on the northwestern side of the reef. At first these spits are unstable, with storms sweeping right across them. Ultimately they build up above the tide, and birds rest on them adding fertiliser. Drift washes ashore, including seeds of beach grasses and shrubs. Given enough time between cyclones, this new sand cay becomes colonised and stabilised by plants.

Sunshine Coral

# Drowned coasts

A flooded gorge, Charnley River, Kimberley (WA)

## A matter of timing

If people had built 40-storeyed skyscrapers by the beach around the Gold Coast in Queensland 14 000 years ago, only the tops of the buildings would be seen above the waves today. The penthouses would be spots over the horizon 50 kilometres to the east of the coast. Since then the sea has risen 120 m. The extra water has come from the melting of the ice caps after the last Ice Age and from the expansion of the warmer water.

Rising sea levels meant that the Aborigines were driven off the coastal plains a number of times. Along the Arnhem Land coast and in southern New South Wales these events form part of oral traditions.

Bathurst Harbour (Tas)

Horizontal waterfalls, Kimberley (WA)

A classic drowned coast, Hawkesbury River, Broken Bay and Brisbane Water (NSW)

---

# DID YOU KNOW?

## FACTS

▶ The sea reached close to its present level 6000 years ago and has stayed near that level since then.

▶ The Kimberley coastline, a flooded coast, may be the result of a combination of rising seas and the land sinking.

▶ About 125 000 years ago the sea level was 5 m higher than at present.

▶ The rate of rise in sea level after the last Ice Age was about 1 m in 70–80 years and the high tide line advanced at about 2 m per year across the coastal plain.

▶ Twelve-metre tides along the Kimberley coast pour water through narrow gaps to fill valleys in horizontal waterfalls.

▶ There appears to have been a rise of nearly 5 mm per year in sea levels for 1993, 1994 and 1995.

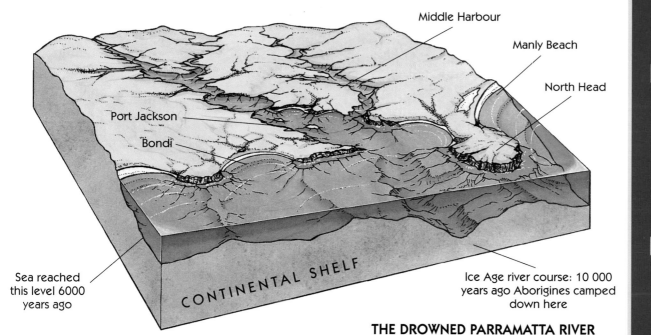

Port Jackson

Bondi

Middle Harbour

Manly Beach

North Head

Sea reached this level 6000 years ago

CONTINENTAL SHELF

Ice Age river course: 10 000 years ago Aborigines camped down here

**THE DROWNED PARRAMATTA RIVER**

## Drowned river valleys, the best harbours

While the sea was lower, rivers cut their beds that much deeper to reach sea level. But when warmer times came, the rising sea flooded the wide coastal plains of the continental shelf. The deepened river valleys were flooded and look like the flooded valleys behind dam walls. Sydney Harbour, the flooded Parramatta River, Broken Bay, Bathurst Harbour, King George Sound, and Twofold Bay are fine examples of drowned river valleys around Australia's coast.

Bathurst Harbour (Tas)

Sydney's harbour, Port Jackson, is the drowned Parramatta River

▶ Sandbars are built by waves pushing sand into a bank. If the wind changes, the end of the bank becomes hooked in shape and is called a recurved spit.

▶ The largest Australian coastal lagoons are the Coorong, the Gippsland Lakes, the Myall Lakes, Wallis Lake, Lake Macquarie, and the Tuggerah Lakes.

▶ Some lagoons have two layers of water: a bottom layer of salt water with fresh water resting on top, both with different species of fish.

▶ Swamp oaks and paperbarks have their roots in only the freshwater swamp soil.

▶ Sandspits and bars tie many islands together to form long sand islands protected by headlands which are the old rocky islands, e.g., Fraser Island, Qld, the world's largest sand island.

MODELLING IN SAND

# Bars and coastal lagoons

Two coastal lagoons, Merimbula (NSW)

Sea, sand barrier and a lagoon, Prion Bay (Tas)

There are many rips and currents in coastal waters that depend on factors such as tides and prevailing winds. As sand is swept along the beach, grains are rolled or picked up in the turbulent water and moved. Where the water is quiet the sand settles. The movement of water and sand creates new coastal features.

Spit and river, Cape York (Qld)

As the sea rises and floods the river valleys, the ridges form headlands and islands. Bays run far inland. Most of the continental coastline has currents running along it which are strong enough to cause the sand to drift in the same direction. Sand is swept around the headland by a current which cuts across the bay mouth. Some sand is pushed in to quiet water behind the headland and sinks. This gradually builds a sandbar.

River entrance and bars (Qld)

The shallower water over the sandbar causes waves to break. These waves help to push more sand onto the sandbar from the supply moving in the current. The sandbar

Bar formation, Lake Eyre (SA)

**FORMATION OF A COASTAL BARRIER**

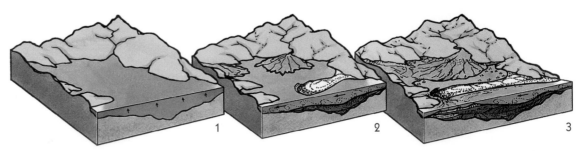

1. Sea level rises  2. Currents transport sand down the coast  3. Sand is deposited in quiet waters, forming a lagoon

Recurved spits, Shark Bay (WA)

Vegetated recurved spits (WA)

A tidal entrance, Jervis Bay (NSW)

A coastal lagoon (NSW)

A filled lagoon (NSW)

Coastal lagoons, Shark Bay (WA)

breaks the surface and becomes a sandspit which continues to grow almost cutting off the bay. Rivers running into the lagoon behind the spit keep a channel open to the sea. Most silt brought in by the rivers settles on the bed of the lagoon, slowly filling it.

The lagoon becomes a salt marsh, then a freshwater swamp, and ultimately a part of the coastal plain. It has rich soils covered first with paper barks and/or swamp oaks and finally a eucalypt forest or, in the tropics, a rainforest.

Rising sea levels can rapidly reverse the process until a new sand barrier, a buffer against the sea, is created. This changing landscape is a rich aquatic and wildlife habitat.

Dunes encroaching on lagoons (Qld)

ALLAN FOX

# Beaches and dunes

Ocean beach, Byron Bay

Beach and dunes, Cape Arid National Park (WA)

The sea has moved backwards and forwards many times across the continental shelf in response to the Ice Ages over the past million years. The waves and currents of the rising sea swept the sands inshore off the shelf, and the longshore drift* spread the sand around the new coastlines. The coastal beaches of today are the result. In many places, onshore winds have heaped sand from dry beaches into dunes parallel to the beach.

## Waves – beach builders and wreckers

Far out across the ocean a steady wind increases in strength from the south-east. The surface is ruffled. Swells begin to form, sweeping towards the coast of Australia. As a wave begins to drag on the sea bed in shallower water, the crest rises, increases its steepness and breaks forward to produce the surf.

Turbulence caused by the breaking waves stirs the sand on the bottom of the sea and sweeps it up the beach. So long as the water is not too turbulent, the sand will be dropped higher up the beach. If the waves approach the beach at an angle, the sand will also move along the beach.

Beach with angled wave approach, Merimbula (NSW)

Water sweeping up the beach returns as swash*. Where the returning waters collect as a mass, their speed will wash a trench in the sea bed, and the resulting current is called a rip. Where the water runs rapidly back down a steep beach, the waves collapse as they meet the beach and returning water. These waves are dumpers.

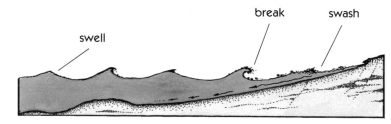
Swash zone on Whalebone Bay beach, Fitzgerald River National Park (WA)

Parallel coastal dunes, Cape York (Qld)

Dune blowout, Fitzgerald River (WA)

Dunes, head of the Great Australian Bight

Storms and undersea earthquakes can stir up massive waves. Storms battering the coast with masses of high waves keep the sand stirred, and huge volumes of water rushing back down the beach carry beach sand to deposit it as a bar offshore where the water is not so turbulent. The beach is eroded. Beach and dunes are sometimes completely swamped by huge storm waves at high tide. As the storm dies and the seas become more settled, the waves break up the bar and the sand is mostly returned to the beach.

The beach is a very efficient shock absorber which must have room to work. Human interference in building breakwaters almost always upsets the natural system.

Onshore winds carry sand inland, building streamlined dunes which are home to plants: twiners first, including creeping grasses, then low-growing plants and shrubs, many especially adapted to growing in salty conditions, and, in the shelter of the swale* behind the frontal dune, trees such as forms of banksia, eucalypt and paperbark.

**BEACH AND DUNES**

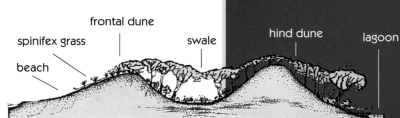

swell    break    swash    spinifex grass    frontal dune    swale    hind dune    lagoon    beach

Red Mangrove

ENTER THE RIVERS
# Estuaries

Mudflats and mangroves and a crocodile habitat at the estuary of the McArthur River (NT)

**Estuaries, the parts of rivers which are tidal, have always attracted humans because there is access to the sea. Brisbane, Perth, Melbourne, Sydney, Adelaide and Hobart all became ports because they were built on river estuaries. Estuaries are also the sections of rivers which collect the sediments and nutrients which run down the river system. This means that these fertile areas are also very rich food-producing areas for plants, animals and humans.**

Water seeks the lowest level – it will always run downhill. The lowest level for most rivers is the sea. Fresh water carrying tiny quantities of salt and, after rain in the headwaters, fine mud particles, reaches the sea and mixes with salt water.

Usually the waters near river entrances are running quietly and, on the out-running (ebb) tides, are almost still. A combination of still waters and salt affecting the clay in the mud causes the mud to sink. Where there are river bends this always happens most rapidly on the inside of the curve.

The action of tides has a large effect on estuaries too. In the Kimberley and at Kakadu, tides may rise 10 m, moving vast quantities of water up and down the estuary as far as 100 kilometres or more each day. Mud is kept suspended in the turbulent water. In the wet season, floods force the muddy water over the banks and the mud settles on the floodplain.

54

Estuary, Nadgee River (NSW)

Along the southeast coast, where tides are 1–2 m, but where there are strong currents pushing sand up or down the coast, sand becomes caught up in the tidal waters moving in and out of the estuary. A series of sand banks forms across the estuary mouth. Tides moving in fan the sand into the river mouth; tides moving out fan sand out into the sea. This is why many estuaries are shallower at the mouth than upstream. Seagrass, mangroves and casuarinas stabilise the new mud- and sandflats.

Mud settles and fills an estuary, Kimberley (WA)

Estuary, Red Rock (NSW)

# FACTS

▶ Mangroves and paperbarks stabilise and protect estuaries from high winds and seas.

▶ Saltwater crocodiles might be better called estuarine crocodiles, as they can survive in the sea, in estuaries or in fresh water.

▶ To keep many estuaries open for shipping, stone breakwaters are built to block sand drifting along the coast. This only works temporarily. Dredges are kept busy clearing the channels. At the Gold Coast (Qld) the drifting sand is pumped around the estuary's mouth.

▶ Human-generated liquid and solid wastes and chemicals dumped into rivers can be trapped in estuaries, making them unusable by people or as animal habitats.

▶ Some canal developments without flow-through water are "sick" estuaries which build up wastes and harbour disease.

Paperbarks

- Deltas, mudflats and estuaries are very important fish nurseries and are some of the most productive places on the planet.

- Mangroves are trees which can survive regular flooding, usually with high salinity, on muddy intertidal* soils low in oxygen.

- Worldwide there are 69 recognised species of mangrove belonging to 20 families of plants. There are 34 species in Queensland and 48 species in the Northern Territory.

- Mangroves occupy about 11 600 km² in Australia.

- Because mangrove species have variable tolerance to salinity, flooding and other conditions, different species colonise different zones along shorelines.

- Estuaries and mudflats will be first areas affected by sea level rises.

RICH AND PRODUCTIVE

# Deltas and mudflats

Mudflats with tide lines in King Sound fed by the Fitzroy, Meda, and Robinson Rivers (WA)

Where the Nile River enters the Mediterranean Sea, a huge green triangle contrasts with the reds and browns of the desert regions and the blue of the sea. This green triangle, which is visible from space, is the flat, lush irrigated land between the many mouths of the Nile, emptying across a vast fan of mud carried from deep within Africa. The triangle is in the shape of the capital form of the Greek letter "Δ", or *delta,* and is the term used to describe this type of river mouth.

## Big wets and gentle seas

Each year, somewhere in northern Australia, tropical cyclones dump immense volumes of water. As it drains onto the coastal lowlands, the brown swirling water is thick with sediment. Here the rivers slow and heavier grains of soil fall to the bed. Fine mud reaches the sea and if the sea is calm, the particles sink. Each year thin layers of mud settle and harden and the mud banks build further and further out to sea. The river builds higher and higher banks along its course until it breaks over the banks and cuts a new course to the sea through the backswamps. A whole network of channels fans out across the growing delta. This muddy channel land is colonised by many species of mangrove.

In the shelter of the Great Barrier Reef, the calm waters of Gulf of Carpentaria, the

Large-leafed Orange Mangrove

Red Mangroves

Avicennia mangrove

Riverine mangrove forest

Effluent channels, salt flats and zones of mangrove species in the mudflats, McArthur River, Borroloola (NT)

Arafura Sea, King Sound and Van Diemen Gulf, great expanses of mudflats and deltas have been able to form. These are rare landforms with complex ecosystems*, which are best preserved when they are declared nature reserves.

Many of Australia's plainlands began forming as prehistoric deltas when huge bays and inland seas were present. The Bulloo, Warrego, Paroo, and Culgoa rivers emptying into northern New South Wales, and the Murrumbidgee, Lachlan, Macquarie and Namoi rivers flooding out across the plains of the Riverina, were the builders of inland deltas which are now vast grassy plains.

Mud is dropped in slow-moving water

Low tide, King Sound (WA)

ALLAN FOX

Ocean currents, mud and mangroves building new land, Hinchinbrook Island (Qld)

57

# Mountains against the sea

### FACTS

▶ Over the past million years the sea level has risen and fallen many times. During the Ice Ages, water was retained on land as ice, and the sea level fell. As the glaciers melted, the sea level rose.

▶ Sea cliffs were carved out during periods of high sea level.

▶ Water does not erode the rocky coast by itself: it is the combination of the sand, grit and boulders, moved by the water, which shapes these coasts.

▶ Blowholes are rock formations where the sea rushes into caverns and forces water and air out through a hole punctured in the roof.

A headland of slates, Whalebone Bay, Fitzgerald River National Park (WA)

The sea is forever on the move, its body being shunted here and there by currents and its surface pushed by the wind into waves. Sand and mud on the shore absorbs the wild energy of the waves by moving and shifting. Rock, which is immobile, is pounded by the waves and breaks down.

Air, trapped in cracks and hollows in the coastal rocks, explodes with each impact. Soon its pressure bursts the cracks wide open. Loose rubble is rolled about the sea floor. Sand and grit swirl in the surging water, grinding the rocky surfaces. Boulders and pebbles trapped in potholes spin about like drills cutting the holes deeper and wider. The holes join, weakening the rock. Masses of

Soft limestone, Point Campbell (Vic)

Mountains meet the sea at Cape York, Australia's northern tip

Dolerite columns, Cape Raoul (Tas)

58

Sea stacks, the Twelve Apostles, Port Campbell (Vic)

Wavecut notch, Great Australian Bight

Waves cutting the edge of a bench

rock fall from above this wavecut notch*. A sea cliff forms above a growing wavecut bench*. The constant action of the waves breaks down the shoreline rocks.

Each kind of rock – granite, basalt, sandstone, quartzite and limestone – shapes coastal cliffs and headlands according to its resistance to weathering and erosion. Granite coasts, as at Wilsons Promontory in Victoria, are rounded; sandstone coasts, as found near Sydney, have vertical cliffs; slatey coasts, as at Fitzgerald River in Western Australia, are sharp and broken; and volcanic coasts, as at Tasman Island, are columnar. The shape of the coast is determined by the kind of rock.

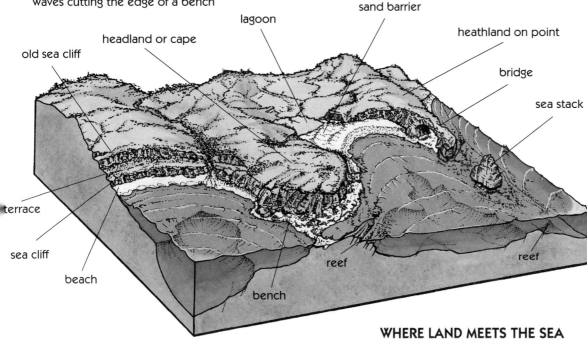
WHERE LAND MEETS THE SEA

ALLAN FOX

## FACTS

▸ Headlands have resisted the erosive action of the sea and their shape is determined by the rock type.

▸ Rocky reefs off headlands show where the headland once stood. Islands are usually the crowns of hills on "drowned" ridges. While the sea was rising, they were headlands.

▸ Most headlands are surrounded by a wavecut bench showing where the cliff once was.

▸ Sea caves are usually the result of cores being washed out of rock folds and volcanic dykes being weathered and eroded out of cliffs by the sea.

▸ Sea stacks are liable to be subject to erosion, known as wavecut, at the point where the waves break against the rocks. This can eventually undermine the rock structure. A good example of wavecut is seen at the Twelve Apostles on the southern Victorian coast.

Pothole

# Dunes of the dry country

A Central Australian dune, scoured by the wind (foreground), moves on

**A TYPICAL DUNE**

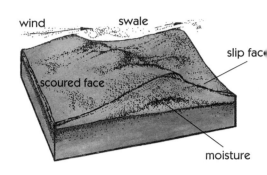

Australia is a low landscape and lies astride the Tropic of Capricorn, the southern mid-latitude desert belt of the world. Deserts and arid landscapes cover 70 per cent of the continent. There are many desert landscapes – mountain, salt lake (salina or playa), tableland, stony desert, riverine* – but perhaps the most common are the dune landscapes. Red iron-oxide-covered sand, cream water-washed sand, grey clay-sand mixes and sparkling gypsum dunes are widely scattered, some near to the sand source, some far away.

Dunes are best studied when the Sun is low in the sky. It is then that the shadows throw the detail of the surfaces into focus, such as the long flowing ripples, tiny images of dunes themselves. Most famous are the parallel dunes of the Simpson Desert. Hundreds of dunes 15–38 metres high run NNW–SSE, two to six every kilometre. Some of them are more than 120 km long. The western faces are quite gentle but the eastern ones are as steep as

Calm weather profile

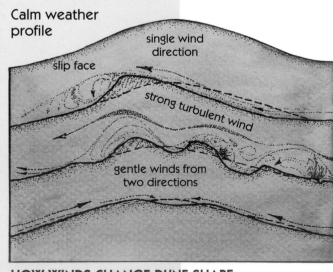

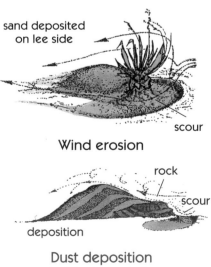

Wind erosion

Dust deposition behind obstacle

**HOW WINDS CHANGE DUNE SHAPE**

The slip face of a desert dune

A drifting dunescape of the reticulate type

Linear, parallel dunes, Simpsons Desert

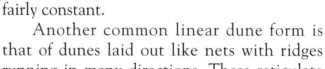

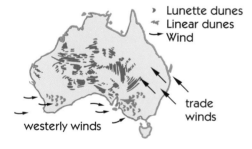
Lunette dunes
Linear dunes
Wind
trade winds
westerly winds

**DUNE PATTERNS IN AUSTRALIA**

loose sand will lie. Here the wind direction is fairly constant.

Another common linear dune form is that of dunes laid out like nets with ridges running in many directions. These reticulate dunes are found near Uluru and are like mazes. Here and there are soft red sand hollows; there are also bays at various levels, and long arms. Most desert dunes are well stabilised by vegetation such as spinifex, grevilleas, acacias and casuarinas. The crests tend to move a few metres back and forth according to the wind shift. Fires destabilise the dunes by burning off the vegetation cover, but usually only for 2 to 3 years.

When the dune systems of Australia are mapped (left) a remarkable total pattern is seen. They encircle the centre of the continent. To the south are semi-circular dunes, the lunettes, which are broad greyish hills of lake floor sediment raised along the eastern shores by the westerly winds.

## FACTS

▶ All major dunefields including Simpsons, Sturts Stony and Strzelecki deserts occur in low, depressed regions where sand collects and where the surface allows free wind-blown sand movement.

▶ Lunettes are dunes shaped like crescent moons. They are formed from dry lake-floor sediment and sand blown from the circular lakes of the southern inland.

▶ The sands of the dunes are composed mainly of quartz. About 1% of grains are magnetite, rutile, zircon, garnet and tourmaline.

▶ Dunes migrate when a consistent wind moves grains upslope to drop them in the protected downwind slope.

▶ Ventifacts are pebbles shaped and polished by wind action. They are found in the swales, between dunes, but mainly they are the remains of old stony hills.

▶ Wind is a transporting agent (i.e., it moves things) but, by itself, it is not an effective agent of rock erosion. The things it carries, such as grains of sand, can act to erode rock, however.

Desert Oak and spinifex, Uluru

A fire in desert oaks

Two years after fire, Uluru

# Uluru and Kata Tjuta

Uluru, a 348-metre-high residual (isolated landform) of sandstone, central Australia (NT)

## FACTS

▶ Both Kata Tjuta and Uluru are remnants of high mountains, which were uplifted 300 million years ago. The rounding of this sandstone is caused by thin plates of surface rock being lifted by the swelling of feldspar. These are then split off by the temperature extremes which cause the rock to expand and contract. Gravity does the rest.

▶ As the rock is slowly reduced in size by erosion, pressure is lifted off underlying layers. These layers rise up from the surface.

▶ In Aboriginal mythology Uluru was originally a great dune upon which the ancestors left their marks of the creation period. There are the myriad holes of the spears of Liru, the poisonous snake; the dish-like cavern where Kuniya the carpet snake hatched her eggs; signs of Kurpani the devil dog-like creature and many more.

Six hundred million years ago, there was a mighty mountain range in what is now called central Australia. From its eroded remnants Uluru and Kata Tjuta were formed.

Uluru, 348 m high, is all that remains of a 300 million year old sandstone range which extends underground some 3 km. The strata are alternately hard and soft, and the grooves and holes that give this large rock its distinctive appearance are the result of erosion from a rainfall which averages 200 mm per year. Uluru stands in a hollow in the dunes caused by encircling scouring winds which result from warm air rising off the rock when the desert air is cold.

West of Uluru the long horizon is broken by a clump of some thirty-six spectacular domes in 40 square kilometres. The largest, Mt Olga, is half as high again as Uluru.

This huge grid of faults and joints has been weathered by water, wind and temperature change, rounding the domes. They enclose a broad valley.

Kata Tjuta is the same age as Uluru but when the sediments were deposited they must have been very close to the mountain source of the massive boulders which make up the conglomerate. The sandstone of Uluru doesn't contain rocks and river pebbles, evidence that it was further away from the range.

The domes of Kata Tjuta across a sea of dunes; Mt Olga is on the left (NT)

# Kakadu

Sandstone outliers and floodplain of the East Alligator River (NT)

The surface of the Arnhem Land Plateau, in the Northern Territory, is covered with a mosaic of colossal boulders, some with caverns, others balancing, but all with intricate patterns caused by weathering and erosion. There are areas where sheets of strata have been removed leaving huge hollows, and in another place an unusual sandstone bridge. The sandstones here are eight times older than those of the Blue Mountains.

As if it were an old skin, the sandstone is peeling back off a lowland of far older metamorphic rocks which carry a vast deposit of uranium. Scattered out from the retreating plateau are outliers, outcrops of resistant sandstone, some like towering islands, others just a pile of boulders on the river floodplains. Where the Alligator rivers have been forced to sweep around the outliers, old and cut-off early channels are now lotus-covered billabongs and lagoons.

Until about 6000 years ago, rising seas flooded lowlands and the broad valley which is now Van Diemen Gulf. Tropical wet seasons carried the silt from eroding Kakadu into the rivers and spread it out from the estuaries. Mudflats and old beaches were built, only to be covered by mangroves, then to be deserted by the sea as shorelines were built further out.

Twin Falls dropping 200 m off the plateau

Lagoons and billabongs, a characteristic of Kakadu

The Kimberley Ranges (WA) meeting the sea

## DID YOU KNOW?

### FACTS

- The Kimberley is more than twice the size of Tasmania.

- The Prince Regent River gorge runs southeast to northwest dead straight along a fault or joint line for more than 100 km.

- Before iron ore was mined in the Pilbara, two Kimberley islands, Cockatoo and Koolan, produced huge volumes of iron ore for Whyalla, Port Kembla and Newcastle steel works.

- The open pit at Koolan Island is now below sea level.

- A very large deposit of high grade bauxite forms Mitchell Plateau, at present covered with palm forests.

- The world's largest operating diamond mine, Argyle, in the east Kimberley, is working a volcanic pipe which was active 1.18 billion years ago.

The ranges of the Kimberley in the northwest of Western Australia are wild and rugged. Ranges of very hard, cream, pink and rusty quartzite run into the sea, usually with a rim of bright green mangroves. A maze of waterways extends into the valleys. Extreme tides race through narrow gaps.

Long fault and joint lines have been widened into gorges like those of the Prince Regent, Mitchell and King George Rivers. The gorges end against sheer smooth red and black walls covered by roaring, foaming water in the wet season and graceful skeins in the dry. Some waterways, such as Bell Creek, drop over a series of giant steps.

The sun-baked pink ranges covered with spinifex and bloodwoods build up from the sea, sometimes as ridges, sometimes domed and capped in places by black basalt covered with richer vegetation. Ultimately the land rises to a plateau with pandanus and paperbark lined creeks.

Windjana Gorge (WA), cut through an ancient reef

The first step into Bell Gorge (WA)

# Nambung

Wind removes the silica sand from between the cemented columns of the Pinnacles at Nambung

## FACTS

▸ The Pinnacles of Nambung are likely to be less than 80 000 years old.

▸ Drifting dunes cover and uncover the Pinnacles in different places from time to time.

▸ When the vegetation protecting dunes is removed by fire, sand is picked up by the wind which sandblasts the columns, etching out the softer parts.

▸ The limestone of the Pinnacles is the same age as the coastal limestones (Tamala Limestone) which run from Shark Bay to Albany.

▸ Some of the early dunes are thought to have reached 300 m high.

▸ In places fossilised roots (roots covered with a skin of limestone) are exposed as sand is blown away. Egg-like fossils of the cases of the weevil pupae *Leptopius* are exposed.

▸ Calcrete is sedimentary rock cemented with calcium carbonate.

For much of the past million and more years, the west of Australia was covered by a shallow sea. These conditions were ideal for the growth of calcareous algae (algae which take up calcium carbonate), shellfish and other invertebrates which produce calcium carbonate. The hard remains of countless dead animals were ground up and washed ashore as a major part of the beaches. This shell grit, mixed with silica sand, was blown into massive dune systems which were colonised by plants.

Beneath the plants a soil began to form. Rainwater is a weak acid which became more acid as moisture seeped through the humus (decayed vegetation). On its way down, this acid water dissolved calcium carbonate which formed a layer of calcrete at the base of the soil.

Plant roots found their way down through cracks in the calcrete and led water deep down. This, along with dissolved calcium carbonate, was absorbed by the columns of sand beneath the blocks of calcrete. The hollows between the columns were left filled with sand which was later removed by wind erosion leaving the standing columns.

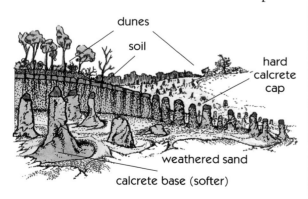

dunes
soil
hard calcrete cap
weathered sand
calcrete base (softer)

**FORMATION OF THE PINNACLES**

Pinnacles of cemented shell grit

# The Grampians

The Grampians (Vic)

- The sandstone Grampians were named by Surveyor-General Thomas Mitchell in 1936 because they reminded him of the Grampians in his native Scotland.

- Ripple marks on some of the rocks were caused by gentle wave action millions of years ago.

- The endangered Brush-tailed Rock-wallaby makes its home in the mountain ranges.

- The varying vegetation types reflect the different soils and locations. Eucalypts dominate the dry slopes which have suffered from frequent fires while tree ferns in the deep gullies are reminders that an ancient rainforest once grew here.

- The Grampian sandstones lie over granite, the great tors of which are seen near Stawell and Ararat, old gold-mining towns.

**Forming the western extremity of the Great Dividing Range is a series of sandstones ranges which run north–south for about 100 km. Here immense parallel faults took place, forcing up the steep eastern escarpments of Mount William, Serra, Wonderland, Mount Difficult, Victoria and the Black ranges. The western faces of the ranges are more gently sloping.**

Millions of years of erosion have fretted out many remarkable sandstone formations. The highest mountain is Mt William (1167 m). With the other peaks of these giant sandstone serrations Mt William looks out over the wide plains of sand to the west and northwest which mark the lands once covered by shallow seas as the Murray Basin filled with sediment.

Rich and varied plant communities harbour more than 1000 species of ferns and flowering plants and provide habitats for animals and birds. The importance of the area has been recognised and it was declared a National Park in 1984.

Weathered sandstone of the Grand Canyon

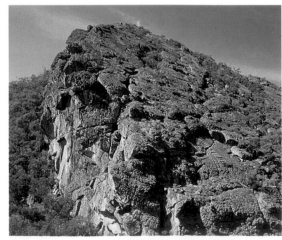

The exposed, steeply eroded eastern slopes

# The Flinders Ranges

River Red Gums grow along the watercourses of the Flinders Ranges which rise from the rolling plains

On the map of South Australia, two sharp features, the "rabbit-eared" shaped gulfs slicing in from the south coast, are the clearest physical features. They indicate a violent history of faults, sinking lands and rising ranges. These ranges, from Mt Remarkable 400 kilometres north to Mt Freeling, are the Flinders Ranges.

They are a mix of resistant golden sandstone and quartzite, grey limey dolomites, red mudstones. In the north about the Gammon Ranges and Arkaroola, minerals produce the green stains of copper, the deep red and brown of iron and manganese, the grey of calcium and much more.

Streams and rivers cut through thousand-metre ranges in wild gorges and canyons lined with some of the finest River Red Gums in the land. Spidery lines outline the oldest fossil remains of animals: sea jellies and sea pens, relics of the sea near Lake Torrens.

But the landforms sculpted by the weather – Wilpena Pound, Chambers Gorge, Brachina Gorge and Parachilna Gorge – are the set pieces here.

Remnants of ancient quartzite sandstone

A dry creek bed near Brachina Gorge

The serrated Arthur Range and glacier modelled landscape, as wild as any in Australia

**Tasmania and mainland Australia were part of the one continent more than 12 000 years ago. Then rising seas from west Bass Strait, driven by the Roaring Forties, flowed over the land and Tasmania became an island. For a period, Aborigines could still make the crossing, but by the time the Dingo arrived in mainland Australia there was no crossing. Tasmanian Tigers and Devils were safe from competition.**

Overlooking the surrounding ranges is the magnificent snow-white quartzite turret of Frenchmans Cap, around which loops the Franklin River. Running south are the jagged peaks of the Frankland Range. Beyond this range once lay the magnificent pink sandy beaches of Lake Pedder, now just another artificially flooded valley surrounded by glacier-carved ranges.

Set in long sweeping curves, the ranges plunge into the Southern Ocean. There are fiord-like inlets at Port Davey and Bathurst Harbour. Bays across which sandbars have formed have locked off lagoons which reflect the cliffs of Pindars Peak and Precipitous Bluff. Dense rainforest covers extensive limestone deposits containing sinkholes and caves.

Sharp mountain peaks, hanging valleys, gorges, moraine lakes, wild rivers, lagoons and fiords all make up the landforms of the southwest.

Sandbar beach, lagoon, ranges and precipitous Bluff

Federation Peak

# The Australian Alps

The upper Snowy valley in winter

About ninety million years ago slow uplift of the eastern highlands began. The stresses and tensions on the granites, slates and other metamorphic rocks were so strong that during the process long faults rent the surface. The Upper Murray, Tumut, Goodradigbee and Murrumbidgee rivers ran straight courses down these faults.

The Ice Ages brought frigid conditions to the Australian Alps. A small ice cap developed with short glaciers carving out U-shaped valleys. There are also large blocks of granite (erratics) lying about which were moved and dropped by the melting ice. The remaining high peaks of the Bogong High Plains in Victoria have resisted further erosion because of their hard basalt caps. Hedley Tarn in the Snowy Mountains lies amongst a series of rubble banks or moraines pushed down the valley by glacial ice.

The upper Snowy valley in summer; most years, the snow drifts last beyond December

## FACTS

▶ Mt Kosciusko is Australia's highest mountain at 2228 m. In the past there were much higher mountains on the continent; the great volcanoes of Mt Warning and Mt Kaputar are just two.

▶ Fossils buried under recent lava flows include leaves of forms of beech and eucalypt trees, pollens and mosses, showing that at the time of eruption the mountains were covered with a warm temperate rainforest.

▶ The heaviest snowfalls occur in late winter in weather which sweeps in from the southwest. Some drifts have been measured in hollows at 30 m deep.

▶ The mountains within Bogong National Park in Victoria, with peaks up to 1986 m, are the remnants of ranges with heights up to 5000 m.

▶ Within 100 years, the removal of ground cover by grazing sheep on the Main Range of Mt Kosciusko caused the erosion of over 1 m of soil from parts of Mt Twynam. It will take about 300 years to return to pre-sheep soil depth.

## FACTS

▶ The Willandra Lakes system was formed over the past 2 million years.

▶ There are five inter-connected dry lake basins varying from 600 to 35 000 ha in area.

▶ The lakes dried out progressively from south to north becoming more saline as rainfall diminished.

▶ The base of the lunette at Lake Mungo is orange-red sand more than 50 000 years old. The middle layer is clean sand topped by a brown sand layer which is partly soil formed when the lakes were full between 50 000 and 19 000 years ago. The top layer is mainly grey clay sand from the lake beds.

▶ Willandra Lakes are within a World Heritage area of great significance protecting a richness of evidence of Aboriginal prehistory and wildlife evolution.

# Willandra Lakes

The lunette dunes at Lake Mungo have been built in at least four stages, each of a different colour

There was a time when the Lachlan River in New South Wales carried much more water along with silt from the southern highlands. It carried so much that the river built a broad delta and plains of sediment. A number of channels swept southwest but two were most important. The present Lachlan River meandered to the south of the delta to meet the Murrumbidgee, while the Willandra ran its course westwards across the delta then south to the Murray River.

As the Willandra wandered and laid down its silt, a number of broad shallow depressions were formed. These became linked to the river during flood times. The Willandra chain of lakes began their life. Waters came and went as the Ice Ages changed the climate. While they were full, winds whipped up waves which rounded off the shorelines. There were sandspits, beaches of small pebbles and low beach dunes. The lakes and surrounding country were a very rich habitat for animal and plant life.

There were many long periods of drought and no water. The Willandra does not appear to have run its full length for 14 000 years or more. Prevailing westerly winds have moved the dune sands and clay from the lake beds to form the massive lunettes.

Dust storms rage across Lake Mungo

Water and wind erosion exposes the ancient fossils

# The Blue Mountains

The Three Sisters against Mt Solitary and the blue haze of Kings Tableland

About 200 million years ago the area around the Blue Mountains in New South Wales was a vast bay. To the west and south were high mountains being worn down by rain and wind. Large rivers ran into this bay from the mountains and carried sand, mud and pebbles until sedimentary beds were kilometres deep. Then, very slowly, the bed of the sea began to rise, shedding the water. The sand had become layers of sandstone, and the mud had become shale. New rivers then carved out valleys, gorges and canyons that visitors from the world over come to admire today.

Roads and railways have conquered the walls by climbing the three great steps to Katoomba and staying on top of the plateau, which is steadily being eaten away by the Wollondilly, Cox's, Grose and Colo Rivers. To look across the Grose to the mighty walls of Mt Banks, with its protective cap of basalt, is to look at 200 million years of geological history written in layer upon layer of horizontal sandstone. This story from Perry's Lookdown is repeated at Govetts Leap and Echo Point.

While the Blue Mountains landscapes are dominated by their shining walls they get their name from the bluish haze generated by the forest vapours.

Sandstones butt against older lands, Kanangra Walls

71

# The Great Barrier Reef

Masthead Island in the Capricorn Group. Note the edge of living coral, the sandflat and the vegetated cay

**The Great Barrier Reef is the largest coral reef, or series of coral reefs, in the world. It stretches for about 2000 km down the coast of Queensland from the tip of Cape York at about 100 km offshore.**

Reef building corals will only flourish in warm ocean waters (20–30°C), at depths of 2–15 metres. Corals will grow, but not as well, to a depth of about 60 metres. Ideal reef building conditions on the broad continental shelf off the coast of Queensland include currents that carry the corals' planktonic food.

Algal plants are a critical part of reef building and strong sunlight through clear water is essential. Water dirtied with mud or chemicals, or which becomes too deep as a result of the rise of the sea, will cause the death of the reef.

At night, the coral reef, which feels like hard rock during the day, becomes a world of tiny bodies and stinging tentacles swaying in the currents taking living food particles from the water.

Feather Stars: part of the galaxy of reef life

Gorgonians and soft corals on the reef slope

# Fraser Island

Indian Head, Fraser Island

Fraser Island in southern Queensland is the world's largest sand island. Over the past million years the sea level has risen and fallen several times. At low levels, a broad continental shelf was exposed as a coastal plain. This immense island was built with huge deposits of sand which originated in sediments eroded from the Great Dividing Range.

Sand drifted northwards, pushed along by nearshore currents and longshore drift driven by southeasterly winds. High volcanic rocky islands underlying Indian Head, Waddy Point and Sandy Cape were tied by spits to Double Island Point, trapping sand and building dunes on the spits. The rising and falling sea levels have swept sand in off the shelf to be added to the growing mass. Seeds, blown by the wind, washed up by the ocean or deposited in the droppings of birds, germinated and thrived.

Lakes and lagoons were closed off within the dune system at various times. Flat areas between dunes became deep bogs packed with plants. Sand drifted across the bogs, bedding them tightly down to form coffee-coloured rock. Lake beds were sealed and became perched lakes when sea levels fell.

Lake McKenzie, a typical perched lake

Rainforest at Wanggoolba Creek, Central Station

# Biodiversity

Black Wallaroo

Short-eared Rock-wallaby

Nourlangie Rock, Kakadu National Park (NT)

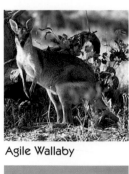
Agile Wallaby

White-bellied Sea-Eagle

Intermediate Egret

Red-winged Parrot

Oenpelli Rock Python

## Nourlangie Rock: a tropical landscape

**A series of great sandstone outliers of the Arnhem Land Plateau in the Northern Territory stand like islands across the Alligator Rivers floodplains.**

The Nourlangie area, pictured above, provides seven major habitats. The sandstone bluff houses four. On top is a very broken **plateau (1)** with very deep rifts and fallen boulders. Pockets of sandy soil grow spinifex tussocks and heath with a few stunted trees. The **cliffs (2)** are terraced and, added to the vegetation on the clifftops, are some areas where water seeps on to rock ledges, **seepages (3)**, with ferns and grasses. **Caverns (4)** exist and some deep rifts. Immediately below the cliffs are immense rock falls with tall eucalypts between the rocks shading the caverns.

A broad skirt of **monsoon woodland (5)** rich in fruiting plants, and ground storey shrubs and grasses cover the footslopes of the bluff.

The **wetland (6)** is seasonal, producing a mass of plants such as spike rushes and lilies. Vast numbers of invertebrates and fish move in from linked deep-water billabongs. **Forests (7)** of paperbarks and freshwater mangroves provide shaded cover on the grassy verges.

Snake-necked Turtle

Masked Rock-frog

Freshwater Long-armed Prawn

Archer-fish

PHOTOS THIS PAGE IAN MORRIS

Swamp Wallaby

Red-necked Wallaby

Eastern Grey Kangaroo

Brush-tailed Rock-wallaby

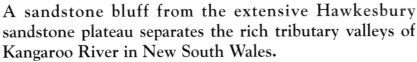

Wedge-tailed Eagle

Gang-gang Cockatoo

White-faced Heron

Koala

Common Brushtail Possum

## Kangaroo Valley: a temperate landscape

**A sandstone bluff from the extensive Hawkesbury sandstone plateau separates the rich tributary valleys of Kangaroo River in New South Wales.**

There are seven habitats numbered in the photograph below. The sandstone is infertile and lacks trace elements. The dry **sclerophyl woodland (1)** of the tops has a very diverse ground storey including waratahs and rich honey-producing plants. The **cliffs (2)** are rifted with some terraces and caverns.

Below the cliffs is a deep, well drained soil enriched by shale. A **tall sclerophyl forest (3)** is on the drier slopes with tree ferns and heavy understorey. Downslope more moisture produces a **temperate rainforest (4)** with Coachwoods and heavily fruiting Lillipillies.

Out in the main valley is an artificial farm habitat of **grassland (5)** with River Oaks and Rough-barked Apples along the creek and river. The creek is seasonal and the river has **permanent waterholes (6)**. **Farm dams (7)** usually support a limited range of aquatic plants and animals.

Each habitat has many hundreds of organisms interacting with the environment and with each other in ways which are not yet fully understood.

Kangaroo Valley (NSW)

Sugar Glider

Black Duck

Where do they live? The habitats of the animals pictured are described and numbered in the text as follows:

Swamp Wallaby 3, 4
Red-necked Wallaby 1, 3
Eastern Grey Kangaroo 1, 3, 5
Brush-tailed Rock-wallaby 2, 3
Wedge-tailed Eagle 1, 2, 3, 5, 6
Gang-gang Cockatoo 1
White-faced Heron 6, 7, 5
Koala 1, 3
Common Brushtail Possum 1, 3, 4, 6
Sugar Glider 1, 3
Black Duck 6, 7

Living landscapes provide for our recreation

Like all other animals, humans are dependent on the Sun and the plants for survival. Plants are the producers of the living world; animals the consumers. Plants are almost the only things which can bring together gases, water and minerals to make living material upon which animals feed.

These living systems of landscape, Sun, plants and animals are the ecosystems: the communities of living things and the ways in which they live and react to each other and their environments. They exist in often fragile and complex relationships to each other, and a great danger to this delicate system is human interference.

We have been careless with many precious landscapes:

Living landscapes provide for our food and water supplies

Living landscapes provide the places for our homes

gully erosion due to clearing of vegetation

ALLAN FOX

The Australian landscape and ecosystems offer endless variety of interest and challenge. Landscapes are alive. They are more than something to look at. Landscapes must be understood. We are all inseparably part of the landscape and it is part of us.

Understanding is the key to wise management of natural resources. Humans are the most powerful species on Earth. We influence what will live and what will become extinct. Humans have caused much damage to the earth and its plants and animals. There is still much to learn, but we now know better than ever how we should act and why we should care.

Living landscapes provide the only resources of biodiversity

# Glossary

**algae.** Simple non-flowering, stemless water plants.

**asthenosphere.** The hot, plastic zone 70–200 km below the Earth's surface.

**backswamp.** The marshy area on a floodplain lower than the natural levees confining the river.

**bacteria.** Simple organisms which cause things to ferment or rot, or cause disease.

**basalt.** A common dark, fine-grained volcanic rock found in lava flows.

**base level.** The level below which a stream cannot erode, i.e., sea level. Lakes form temporary base levels.

**batholith.** A large body of igneous rock, e.g., granite, that rises through the Earth's crust.

**bed load.** Material such as gravel, pebbles, etc., swept along the bed of a stream.

**calcite.** A mineral, calcium carbonate.

**catchment.** The area in which rainfall collects to feed a river or lake on the surface or underground.

**conglomerate.** A coarse-grained sedimentary rock with pebbles and boulders in it.

**continental plate.** A massive slab of the Earth's crust embedded in the lithosphere which moves over the plastic asthenosphere.

**continental shelf.** The submerged margin of a continent usually to a depth of 120 m.

**corallite.** The coral skeleton of a marine polyp.

**diatomaceous earth.** Beds of silica 'skeletons' from masses of diatoms, microscopic algae living in mineral-charged waters.

**dolerite.** A medium grained igneous rock.

**dyke.** An angled sheet of igneous rock formed when magma from the interior of the Earth has forced its way towards the surface and has cooled and solidified.

**ecosystem.** Communities of living things and the ways in which they live and react to each other and their environments.

**exfoliation.** Weathering of rock which causes 'skins' to break from the surface, as from granite tors.

**feldspar.** A mineral group based on an aluminium silicate framework and including a mix of calcium, sodium and/or potassium.

**frontal dune.** The beach dune fronting the sea.

**gneiss.** A metamorphic rock which shows banding and which is rich in quartz and feldspar.

**groundwater.** Water below the surface generally occurring in spaces in rocks and soil.

**gypsum.** A mineral of evaporated lakes and swamps composed of calcium sulphate with water; glistening crystalline sheets.

**igneous rock.** Rock formed by the cooling of molten silicate minerals (magma) as in volcanic rocks or granite.

**intertidal.** Describing the area between the high and low tide marks.

**invertebrate.** An animal lacking a backbone or spinal column.

**larvae.** An early stage in the life cycle of an animal.

**levee, natural.** The build-up of a stream's banks due to silt being deposited during floods.

**longshore drift.** The process which moves sediment along a beach in a zig-zag pattern.

**magma.** Rock, heated to such a high temperature that it becomes liquid or molten, rising from the planet's interior.

**mesa.** A flat-topped hill usually capped with a layer of resistant rock.

**metamorphic rock.** Rock which has changed under intense pressure or heat, such as shale to slate.

**palaeo-river.** An ancient river system frequently covered with later sediments and/or marked by chains of salt lakes or River Red Gums.

**planktonic.** Consisting of drifting or floating organic marine life.

**planula.** An early stage in the life cycle of the coral polyp.

**plastic.** A condition of rock that occurs when it is subjected to intense heat and/or under intense pressure, and it becomes pliable, like plasticine.

**playa.** A depression in a desert basin which sometimes holds water becoming a temporary lake.

**plug.** A resistant spire of volcanic rock; a cast of a volcanic pipe exposed by erosion.

**polyps.** Small marine animals having tube- or cup-shaped bodies, e.g., hydras, sea anemones and corals.

**quartzite.** A sandstone recrystalized by heat and pressure.

**reticulate dunes.** Dunes which lie in a net-like pattern.

**riverine.** Having to do with a river or river bank.

**salina.** A desert depression, caked with salt, which sometimes holds water becoming a temporary lake.

**sandstone.** A sedimentary rock comprised of freshwater, marine or wind-blown sands.

**schist.** A medium-grained metamorphic rock with strong shining skin-like layers caused by the alignment of mica, talc and chlorite.

**sediment.** Matter, such as gravel, sand and mud, that is transported by wind and water.

**shale.** Rock from sedimentary mud or sand deposited in basins.

**shield volcano.** A shield-shaped mountain built from layers of fluid basaltic lava.

**silica.** Silicon dioxide, principle constituent of sandstone and other rocks.

**slate.** A fine-grained metamorphic rock that splits into smooth plates.

**strata.** Layers of sedimentary rock.

**swale.** The valley between dunes.

**swash.** The rush of water sweeping up or down the beach from breaking waves.

**thaw.** The melt of snow or ice as temperature rises.

**tillite.** Sediment from glacial action bedded into a rock similar to conglomerate.

**tsunami.** A seismic sea wave caused by earthquakes, faulting or undersea landslips.

**tuff.** A fine-grained rock like sandstone formed from volcanic ash.

**volcanic pipe.** The pipe-shaped formation which supplies magma to a volcano.

**water table.** The upper edge of the zone under the surface where all spaces in rock and soil are filled with water.

**wavecut bench.** A terrace of shoreline rock eroded at the tidelines by wave action.

**wavecut notch.** A notch cut by wave action at tide level undermining a cliff.

# Map

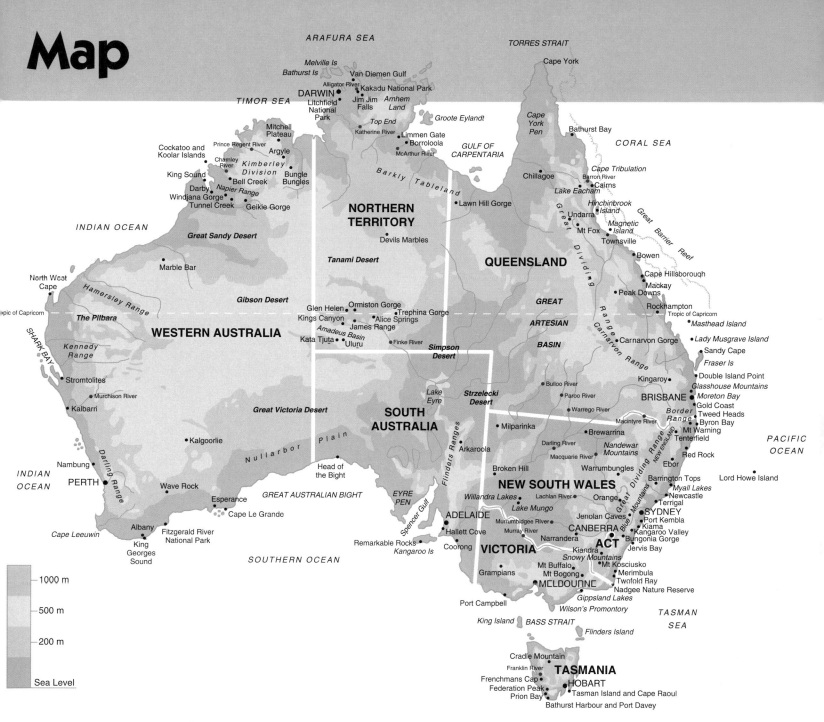

## Recommended further reading

CHAPMAN, D.M., GEARY, M., ROY, P.S. AND THOM, B.G. 1982. *Coastal Evolution and Coastal Erosion in New South Wales.* Coastal Council of NSW, Sydney.

HAMBLIN, W.K. AND CHRISTIANSEN, E.H. 1995. *Earth's Dynamic Systems, 7th edn.* Prentice Hall, Englewood Cliffs.

STRUCKMEYER, H.I.M. AND TOTTERDELL, J.M. (COORD. BMR PALAEOGEOGRAPHIC GROUP). 1990. *Australia, Evolution of a Continent.* AGPS, Canberra.

SUTHERLAND, L. 1995. *The Volcanic Earth.* Univ. of NSW, Sydney.

TWIDALE, C.R. 1993. *Australian Landforms.* Blackwell, Melbourne.

WHITE, M.E. 1986. *The Greening of Gondwana.* Reed, Sydney.

WHITE, M.E. 1994. *After the Greening – The Browning of Australia.* Kangaroo Press, Sydney.

FOX, A.M. AND PARISH, S. 1984. *Australia's Wilderness Experience.* Rigby, Adelaide.

## Maps and place guides

Reader's Digest *Atlas of Australia*, 2nd edn.
*Outback Central and South Australia*, 2nd edn.
Reader's Digest. 1993. *Illustrated Guide to Australian Places.*

## Acknowledgements

Photography by Steve Parish and, where credited, Allan Fox and Ian Morris.

First published in Australia by Steve Parish Publishing Pty Ltd
PO Box 2160 Fortitude Valley BC Queensland 4006
© 1997 copyright photography, illustration and text Steve Parish Publishing Pty Ltd
Printed in Hong Kong by South China Printing Co.

ISBN 1 875932 38  0

## Dedication

To my parents who gave me the genes and to Allen Strom who opened my eyes to see. *Allan Fox*

# Index